GOD

&

SPIES

BASED ON A TRUE STORY
TOP SECRET OPERATION

G. M. Matheny

Dedicated to my parents, Frank and Rita Matheny. My dad served in the air force and met my mom in Belfast, Ireland, during WWII.

Honour thy father and thy mother,
as the LORD thy God hath commanded thee;
that thy days may be prolonged,
and that it may go well with thee,
in the land which the LORD thy God giveth
thee. (Deuteronomy 5:16)

Author Garry and wife, Nancy

G. M. Matheny was a navy diver on the nuclear submarine USS *Halibut* SSN 587 and received the Legion of Merit for a special operation. He graduated from Pacific Coast Baptist Bible College in 1979 and has authored four books. He and his wife, Nancy, were called to the mission field, and they've served as missionaries in Romania since 1991.

Foreword

Garry Matheny is a friend and a fellow preacher. He served in the US Navy as an elite saturation diver. He was involved in one of America's most important (and dangerous) clandestine operations.

Garry does a marvelous job of weaving recently declassified information regarding the NSA analyst who betrayed the operation to the Russians and his own eyewitness account.

If you like good old-fashioned American bravado, espionage and American history, you will enjoy this book.

Pastor Marvin McKenzie
Puyallup, Washington

Preface

Originally I did not want to be in the navy or become a diver. But after five years on active duty, I was begging God to let me be one of the daredevil divers, jockeying to make a top-secret dive in Siberia.

I was privileged to have been attached to the nuclear submarine USS *Halibut*. I was on board during her second deployment in 1974 and her only deployment in 1975, the one in which this account is centered.

Operation Ivy Bells

The CIA headed up a joint operation with the NSA (National Security Agency) and the US Navy, code-named Operation Ivy Bells. The CIA articles that are now declassified, and approved for release, will provide the classified portions of the operation.

There are books, TV, YouTube, and newspapers that have given information on Operation Ivy Bells, calling it "Undersea Espionage" and naming the USS *Halibut* the "Spy Sub"—and all prior to the declassification by the CIA. But these were written after the Russians found out about it.

However, one major newspaper wrote about the operation even before we made our dives. The *New York Times*, on Sunday, May 25, 1975, said on the front page that US "submarines were able to plug into Soviet land communication cables strewn across the ocean bottom and thus were able to intercept high-level military messages and other communications considered too important to be sent by radio or other less secure means." This article was written two months before our sub left port for the operation. We divers had read this article back then, and when we asked about it, the navy told us that if the government confronted the newspaper, it might draw the attention of the Russians.

Though others know about this mission, there are several developments that have never been covered. Also, I know of no other account given by the divers who participated in Operation Ivy Bells or of anyone who was attached to the USS *Halibut*.

All Scripture quotations are from the King James Version of the Bible (KJV). Because of the many items the general public will not be aware of, I have chosen to explain them one at a time rather than slow the story down and try to explain them all at once.

Disclaimer

I will relay the storyline from my undocumented personal recollection and the CIA releases. I will differentiate between what

I saw or did from what I was told or heard. The accounts of Ronald Pelton, the man who betrayed Operation Ivy Bells, as given in the CIA releases, are accurate, but the timeline has been changed to fit this story. The problem that arose on the second water entry, happened, but took place on the second saturation dive. Accounts of the briefings are conflated from different meetings. The accounts of the Soviets, unless in the CIA declassified releases, are speculative or dramatization, including the Soviet Destroyer.

Pictures of the inside of the submarine are from the USS *Blueback* 581. Though she was a diesel sub, she was constructed during the same time period as the USS *Halibut* 587, and the USS *Blueback* has much the same look on the inside as the *Halibut*. The *Blueback* is now at the Oregon Museum of Science and Industry. Her classified equipment was taken off before being turned into a museum.

For privacy, I have changed the names of those on board the USS *Halibut*. The crew of the *Halibut* was not told the name of the other submarine that rendezvoused with us, so I have given her the name USS *Stingray*.

Declassified

Grateful acknowledgment to the CIA for releasing this material, which gives the name of the operation, what we did, where we did it, how we did it, and the results. CIA releases are dated from 2011–2013. However, they were not available for viewing until the "Document Creation Date: December 22, 2016."

In March of 2006, I sent a Freedom of Information Act (FOIA) request to the Office of Naval Intelligence (ONI) asking if I could write about Operation Ivy Bells. My request was denied, but they recommended I appeal to the Department of the Navy, office of the Judge Advocate General (JAG). This I did and acknowledged to them that I had signed a nondisclosure act. I asked why others who worked for the government on this operation and who had also signed nondisclosure acts could publish books written in the first person (not hearsay) about Operation Ivy Bells. Their response was "Your appeal also poses questions concerning your nondisclosure obligations. This office's authority is limited to appeals under the FOIA/Privacy Act (PA) for the Department of the Navy. Your questions fall outside my cognizance." This was dated 22 May 2006, Department of the Navy, office of the Judge Advocate General.

Naval officer John P. Craven was the chief scientist of the Special Projects Office of the US Navy. He has a bachelor's degree (Cornell University), a master of science degree (California Institute of Technology), a PhD (University of Iowa), and a law degree (George Washington University). He guided the navy's undersea special projects operations during the Cold War, and we owe him a debt of gratitude for his service. He oversaw the conversion of my submarine the USS *Halibut* that equipped her with many of the features that she used in our special operation.

In his book *The Silent War: The Cold War Battle Beneath the Sea*, published March 15, 2001, he talks about the project I was involved in. On pages 278–279, he said,

"Pelton would betray how the navy had tapped Soviet underwater communications cables, including the crucial role of saturation diving in those operations." I was grateful to naval officer John P. Craven for writing about this back then and giving an account of our operation that was more than hearsay. This gave credibility to our operation, as John Craven was personally involved, and it could not be swept under the rug as some fantastic story.

I emailed John P. Craven a few times and received two emails back from him. One dated 22 March 2006, in which he talked about writing his book, he wrote, "I have to walk a very fine line." How was he able to do this? Besides being a scientist, he was also a lawyer. He told me, "That is not to say you should not attempt to write a biography that publicizes the heroism of the men of *Halibut* in the conduct of perilous and important missions for the United States." He then added, "You should also know that this letter to you is not off the record and you may use it or not use it as you wish. Best of luck, Craven."

On October 2, 2017, I called the CIA and asked about their declassified information in the Freedom of Information Act Electronic Reading Room, which includes Operation Ivy Bells and Ronald Pelton, the man who betrayed it. During that conversation, I told them I had not been a member of the CIA but was involved in a classified operation the CIA headed up, but now their Electronic Reading Room listed this operation as declassified. I was told that everything on their site is in the public domain and I could write about it.

On October 16, 2017, I received a CIA response to my email: "Thank you for your email. You may freely link to the Central Intelligence Agency website or any of its content. We ask only that you identify that the source of the link is to a Central Intelligence Agency internet resource. Please visit the notice page on our website which addresses this issue."

Their "notice page" that I was referred to said, "Central Intelligence Agency website is in the public domain and may be reproduced, published or otherwise used without the Central Intelligence Agency's permission."

Table of Contents

Thank You!

A special word of thanks to *Halibut*'s crew, who brought us to the dive station and then home safely and worked professionally in all their responsibilities.

David therefore sent out spies.
(I Samuel 26:4)

"There was an espionage submarine called *Halibut.*" John P. Craven

Introduction
Soviet Territorial Waters, Summer 1975

CIA Release

"Ivy Bells ... an undersea cable linking one part of the Soviet Union to the other across the Sea of Okhotsk, was bugged by a device set out by a submarine. A submarine pulled near it and frogmen went out and attached a device ..." (Declassified and Approved for Release 2011/12/21, CIA-RDP90-00965R000100310013-6)

Nuclear Submarine USS *Halibut*, Depth 400 feet.

Two US Navy saturation divers are in the water—Red Diver (Matheny) and Yellow Diver (Farinella). Matheny, speaking through diver communication, says, "Topside, Red Diver: Yellow Diver is working on the last tapping clamp, and we should be wrapping up here in about five minutes."

Inside the USS *Halibut*, at the Main Diver Control station, master diver responds, "Our spooks tell us they have a good strong signal off that Russian cable. Great job, guys! There's going to be some happy people back in the States."

Outside the sub the visibility in the water is less than five feet in the blackness of the frigid sea. Matheny is smiling and looking at the Russian amplifier with its strong signal that made it possible for the taps, when the unexpected happens, and his face lights up in red. This is from a warning light that is on the inside his face mask. He has lost his heliox gas supply and is now on his emergency return bottle with only minutes left to live.

"Topside, Red Diver. I have a red light!"

"Red Diver, return to dive station."

Sonar man belts out, "Captain, on sonar we picked up a Russian destroyer that is using active sonar pinging into the sea."

Intercom: "This is the captain; go to all quiet." Then *Halibut*'s captain steps over to

Main Diver Control and says, "Diving Officer, tell the divers to get out of the water now!"

"Yellow Diver, Topside: Stop whatever you are doing and return to Dive Station!" The master diver then tells the captain, "Captain, Red Diver, Matheny, is already coming back. He had a red light come on in his helmet."

"How serious is this?" asks Captain Larson.

"He has lost his heliox supply and is now on his emergency return bottle. We're timing him, but if he goes straight back, he should make it."

Pings from the Russian destroyer can be heard by the divers and are growing louder. The pings also affect the communications between the divers and Topside.

"Topside, Yellow Diver: *What's the noise?!*"

"Yellow Diver, Topside: We have a visitor. Get back in as quickly as possible."

Red Diver has all 350 feet of his umbilical cable in the water, and the communication box where the tenders are does not work. He has no way to tell them he has a red light or to help him bring in his umbilical cable.

Red Diver reaches the side of the sub and swims up to the top of the *Halibut*. He goes aft until he reaches the DSRV, which has the dive chamber. He makes it to the first leg of the DSRV but has been dragging all 350 feet of his umbilical cable, which is weighing on him. He then pushes off the first leg of the DSRV but only goes a few feet when his umbilical cord stops moving. Then unexpectedly Red Diver's umbilical jerks him backward, and with a sharp pull!

"What?" says Red Diver to himself.

The tenders in the dive chamber have received word from the Main Diver Control to bring in Red Diver's umbilical cable. But while they are attempting this, Red Diver's cable is ripped out of their hands!

"What's going on?" one of the tenders asks.

Matheny's fins have landed back onto the first leg of the DSRV, which keeps him from sliding back any farther. He then pulls toward him about 30 feet of his umbilical cord and makes a dash for the next leg coming down from the DSRV. The red light is shining in his face reminding him he is running out of time, and the Russian destroyer's pings are increasing in intensity.

He makes it to the next leg of the DSRV, from this position, he can see the light shining down in the water from the entry point back into the dive chamber. He positions himself to push off this last leg of the DSRV. But then, unexplainably, he is again yanked backward and his face mask slams into the leg of the DSRV. Matheny grabs for this leg and clings to it.

Chapter I

Six Years Earlier

I was 18, reckless, and wanted the party life. I owned a brand-new 1968 Cougar with a 428 Cobra jet engine, and I thought, *I look good behind the wheel of this car!*

Is not this a brand plucked out of the fire?
(Zechariah 3:2)

"Spectacular Wreck"

"Everett police officers and firemen worked for 40 minutes extracting the driver from his demolished car." (Front page of the *Everett Herald*, a Washington State newspaper.)

It was 3:00 a.m. I had just left a party and was headed home. I was driving 125 miles per hour, and at that speed the valves floated in the engine—otherwise, I would have been going even faster. I was not in a hurry to get anywhere; I was just foolish.

I lost control as I approached the 41st Street Broadway overpass in Everett, Washington. The car spun out and skidded around sideways, leaving 80 feet of skid marks, and hit the corner of the bridge. At impact, the tires hit the curb and blew out. Fortunately, my head tilted to one side as the car tipped over. So when the bridge tore through the roof, it smashed my left shoulder, instead of my head, and pushed me into the backseat. The force of the crash embedded the car key, which was in the dashboard, into the floor of the car. The accident crushed the car's body, springing its frame into the shape of a banana.

The roof had pinned me into the backseat, and I could not breathe. My only thought was, *I don't want to die.* With my right hand, I pulled myself up to a position where I could get air into my lungs. It took about 30 minutes for the police to arrive, followed by the fire department. Those who found my car thought no one could have survived, so the coroner was also called to the scene. It took 40 minutes for the fire department to pry the door open with their hydraulic rescue tool. Thankfully, I was alone that night; otherwise, someone else would have ended up hurt or dead.

I was taken to the emergency room in the Everett hospital. My tendons were snapped in my left shoulder, my left anklebone was broken and they put my leg in a cast. (I still have an aluminum screw in my ankle to this day—a little reminder of the foolishness of my youth.) And there was one major problem.

During my first few days at the hospital, I lay unconscious most of the time and only occasionally woke up. On the second day I was awakened by a nurse taking my blood pressure—three time in a row! She then ran off and brought the doctor back, who also took my blood pressure. The doctor had me drink something that he said would show up better under an x-ray machine. After the x-ray, the doctor said I had internal bleeding in my left kidney and they were not sure they could stop it.

The doctor called my parents, and they came and spent the night with me. Sometime that night I woke up and saw my dad looking at me with an expression that said, *What am I doing, raising these kids?* He said nothing; he just wore that expression. This was the second wreck I had been in, in just two months. Both wrecks were my fault, my new car was totaled, and now I had hurt my dad.

I said, "Dad, I feel like I have let you down."

"No," he said.

But I had and it bothered me.

I loved my dad and I knew he loved me. He was a hard worker and paid the bills. He had told me years before how he was raised, that my grandfather would get upset for no reason and take him away from my grandmother to "teach her a lesson." My grandmother told me that one time my grandfather took my dad away from her for a year and a half. When my dad came back home, he was wearing the same clothes he'd left in, but his arms and legs where sticking out farther from his shirtsleeves and pant legs because he had grown. On a couple of occasions my dad told us kids he did not want us raised the way he was.

I had been going around doing my own thing, not concerned with, or even considering, others' feelings. My only concern was making myself happy. But in that hospital room, my dad was looking at me and wondering if raising me had been worth it. I didn't like seeing my dad look like that. I decided then to do something that would please him and not me. Without realizing it, I began to obey the

Bible—"Honour thy father." No, this did not save me or forgive my sins, but there is a promise attached to this commandment, found in Deuteronomy 5:16, "that it may go well with thee."

Three days after I was in the hospital, the doctors were able to stop the bleeding in my left kidney. A month later I was discharged, but as soon as I was home, my friends called and wanted to party. Which I did, that night and every night following. One night my parents waited up for me because I came home late, and they were worried. When I walked through the door, my dad hollered at me. Later when I went to bed, I thought about the decision I'd made in the hospital, to try and please my dad instead of myself.

A few months after I was released from the hospital, and the cast on my leg was removed, my dad said, "Garry, you ought to join the Navy Seabees and learn a trade."

"Okay," I said.

"Really?" he asked.

"Yes."

He looked at me surprised but wasted no time in getting me into his truck and driving me down to the navy recruiter. It was something I never would have done on my own. My dad was concerned about me getting hooked on drugs, my circle of friends, and the direction I was going in, which was nowhere! I had wrecked my new car, and I felt like my life was going a hundred miles an hour down a dead-end street. Recklessness has consequences, but I was going to take my chances—until I saw how it affected my dad. So I signed up for the navy, not because I wanted to but to make my dad happy.

Chapter II

National Security Agency (NSA)
Fort Mead, Maryland

CIA Release

"Pelton, a former $24,000-a-year communications specialist at the NSA is on trial in Baltimore on charges of selling sensitive information to the Soviet Union … Pelton was suspected of giving away a highly sensitive NSA program, code-name Ivy Bells …" (Declassified in Part—Sanitized Copy Approved for Release 2013/05/21: CIA-RDP99-01448R000301220035-3)

CIA Release

"Pelton filed for bankruptcy in Baltimore. On his form, he listed having $64,000 in debts and less than $10 in cash assets." (Declassified in Part—Sanitized Copy Approved for Release

NSA

Six NSA cryptologists are in their cubicles, men in suits and ties, women professionally dressed. Ronald Pelton, mid-40s, brilliant cryptologist but poor at financial matters, is worried as he receives a call from one of his creditors. He looks around to see who might be watching him, and says, "How did you get my number?"

"The concern here is not about your phone number—it's your debt."

"Look, I will take care of this, but don't call here again."

Mr. Pelton then hangs up, gathers his composure and courage, and goes to ask his boss for a raise. He passes his coworkers, and outside his boss's office he hesitates, then pushes the door open and goes in. He stands in front of his boss's desk for a moment and then says, "Sir, about that raise. The one I asked you about at the beginning of the month."

His boss smiles and says, "Well, Ronald, we indeed do have something for you. You're being given a promotion with more responsibilities and your own office. I'm sure you will like it better than your cubicle."

"Really? Which office?"

"Second floor, room 33." His boss then hands him a folder, stamped in red "TOP SECRET".

Mr. Pelton looks at it for a moment, and his boss says, "There are several new Russian interpreters coming your way. You'll read about it in your folder. Code name is Ivy Bells."

Pelton laughs. "Ivy Bells—is this a joke?"

His boss shakes his head no.

"About the raise, how much is it?"

"As to the raise, that will come in due time. But for now, you can enjoy your new office."

Pelton is frustrated and asks, "Did you say 'several interpreters'? To get them up to speed on our deciphering equipment will take time. How much time do I have for this?"

"Just get them ready, Ronald. Something is coming our way, and it has been given top priority." As Mr. Pelton walks towards the door, his boss says, "Ronald, you know anything about submarines?"

Mr. Pelton turns back toward his boss and says with indifference, "They go under water."

"They do more than that, Ronald. Go over your file."

Chapter III
Planting a Seed

After surviving boot camp, I ended up at the Seabee base in Davisville, Rhode Island. Seabees are a naval construction battalion for building airbases and camps. I was assigned to Mobil Construction Battalion One, which had just returned from a tour in Vietnam. The base in Davisville had an air base, chow hall, theater, and barracks. I didn't know anyone there, I had no car, no money, and no party life.

One evening when I was returning from the base theater, I saw some Seabees coming out of a small building, and I asked another Seabee about them. He told me it was a weekly Bible study. I had no interest in that and just said, "Oh." But even if I had been interested, I wouldn't have gone, fearing I might get harassed for going to a Bible study. But those who went there did not let that stop them.

A few weeks later, one of the Seabees I had seen going to the Bible study was on a military bus with me. We had just come back from Camp Fogarty, a navy firing range where we practiced shooting the M60 machine gun and M16 rifle. This Seabee had been sitting on a bench seat in the bus, and while the bus was moving, for no apparent reason he came over and sat next to me. And in his hand was an open New Testament. I was very surprised he did this—the bus was almost full of Seabees. The situation felt awkward with some of the Seabees looking at us. Then without any introduction or small talk, he just started with, "Did you know that God loves you?" He read John 3:16: "For God so loved the world that he gave his only begotten Son, that whosoever believeth in him should not perish, but have everlasting life."

I thought, *That doesn't say anything about me.* I turned my back on him and then a moment later I glanced over at him, and he looked dejected. But he had planted God's Word in my heart. That same night, I went over what he had said and realized I was also part of this "world," but still thought, *God doesn't love me.*

Almost two years after the Seabee tried to witness to me on the bus, the thought, for whatever reason, came back to me: *Maybe God loves me like someone loves a phone book with all those names in it, and I am part of the billions on the globe. So in that sense maybe it could be true that God loves me.* But I still did not consider it a personal love that God had for me.

***

What would God have to do to prove his love to you? "But the very hairs of your head are all numbered" (Matthew 10:30). Even your mother does not know how many hairs you have. "How precious also are thy thoughts unto me, O God! How great is the sum of them! If I should count them, they are more in number than the sand" (Psalm 139:17–18). God thinks about you more than anyone. "Greater love hath no man than this, that a man lay down his life for his friends" (John 15:13). Christ loves you so much that He took your place and died for your sins.

Back then I was not sure God existed. I would not say He didn't exist, but I could not say He did. And the only time I talked about God was to use His name in vain. But only believing that God exists does not save anyone; salvation needs to take place. The devils are not atheist, but neither are they saved. "Thou believest that there is one God; thou doest well: the devils also believe, and tremble" (James 2:19).

My car wreck made me realize I was not "Mr. Indestructible." This life, compared to eternity, is only a split second, and I had begun to wonder, *After death, where am I going?* All these thoughts were in my head, including, *If God made me, then He should know how to make me happy*. I started to read the Bible, and though when I first read it, I was not sure that the Bible was God's Word, or even if God existed. Still, "Seek, and ye shall find."

The Bible was different from anything else I had ever read. It boldly declared, "For all have sinned, and come short of the glory of God" (Romans 3:23). It was teaching a different way to heaven than what I had believed. My thought then was, *I am no worse than anyone else, so if there is a God, then He will let me go to heaven.* But I kept reading in the Bible that we could not save ourselves and that we needed Jesus Christ to do this.

When Jesus died, there were two other men who died that day (Luke 23:39–43). There were three crosses: Jesus Christ in the middle and two thieves on each side of him. And Christ took one thief to heaven, but not the other. Do you know what made the difference? They both believed Christ existed, for they both talked to him, but only one of them trusted Christ for salvation. This was the one who recognized he was a sinner, for he said, "We receive the due reward of our deeds." He did not make excuses for his sins but looked to

Jesus. He was not baptized, did not partake of the Lord's table, was not good. He was a thief and had broken the eighth commandment, "Thou shalt not steal." Don't get me wrong, all those good things we should do, but they will never take you to heaven—only God's Son can do this.

The thief on the cross put his faith in Christ. "And he said unto Jesus, Lord, remember me when thou comest into thy kingdom. And Jesus said unto him, Verily I say unto thee, To day shalt thou be with me in paradise" (Luke 23:42–43).

I realized that if I was ever going to get to heaven, I would have to do it God's way. I could not expect God to change His plan of salvation for me, but I could change my beliefs and trust His Son to save me. My faith in Him increased to the point that one evening, in a navy barracks, I also called upon Jesus Christ to come into my soul and be my Savior. "For whosoever [anyone] shall call upon the name of the Lord shall be saved" (Romans 10:13).

Chapter IV
Navy Dive Schools

I did not want to become a diver, but I did, and for the same reason I joined the navy, to please my dad.

I joined the navy as a reservist and had a two-year active-duty obligation. But I kept extending my active-duty time so I could attend three navy diving schools. In all, I served nearly five years on active duty and more than a year reserve time.

The Seabees sent me to a 12-week steelworker class "A" school at Port Hueneme, California. While there I saw a guy filling in a request to become a navy diver. I asked him about it, and he said that if I was interested, I should also put in for it. I was not interested in diving (though now I am proud of it), but I did it for my dad. He used to like watching the TV program *Sea Hunt*, starring Lloyd Bridges. He even said one time, "Garry, we ought to take up diving." Well, he never did, but I did for him, thinking this would make him proud of me and put a smile on his face. Every few months I would write home and tell my parents about my navy schools, knowing it would make them happy. I knew they wanted to be a part of my life.

Author at navy second-class dive school,
Washington, DC

Second-Class Dive School

The navy sent me to second-class dive
school in Washington, DC, a ten-week diving
and salvage school. We made most of our
practice dives in the Anacostia and Potomac
River. There were also dive chambers inside
this navy facility, and they could "press us

down" by adding air pressure inside the dive cambers.

I enjoyed this school and the Washington, DC, area was a fun place. I lived off base with some other navy divers, and I liked visiting the sites: the US capitol, Arlington National Cemetery, Lincoln Memorial and the US Marine Corp Iwo Jima War Memorial.

Indian Ocean

From Washington, DC I spent eight months on the Island of Diego Garcia in the middle of the Indian Ocean. We were the second Seabee battalion to arrive there, and we lived in plywood barracks with only screens for windows. In fact, there was no glass anywhere on the island, and the only inhabitants were us Seabees, 1,000 of us, and no women. It was very hot, with coconut trees everywhere and dozens of crabs, some very large, skittering across the sand. Thankfully, the divers could go diving for fun. Diego Garcia provided the best scuba diving, with coral reefs and an assortment of sea shells.

I and four other navy divers made most of our dives from a barge and a 30-foot motor boat. While there we put in an underwater sewer line (not fun). But our main job was to make 60-foot dives in the harbor to connect the hoses of fuel ships to an underwater pipeline. The fuel was then pumped to shore for the aircraft that landed on the island.

We saw sharks and eels almost daily. Usually the sharks would circle us one time and then swim off. On one dive, I and two other divers stayed topside while two divers made a 60-foot dive. Ten minutes passed, and both divers surfaced early. One climbed up a ladder, and the other was ditching his tanks when we pulled him up out of the water. Shark fins were suddenly on the surface, moving fast through the water. The divers said that these sharks did not circle them as usual but passed between them at close range, and they'd felt threatened.

First-Class Dive School

At first-class dive school, which was also in Washington, DC, we were taught underwater welding, underwater demolition, and mixed-gas dives, called "heliox" (helium and oxygen), for deep dives. This diving school lasted 17 weeks, and one of the more fun projects was raising a ship they had sunk in the Potomac River.

Island of Guam

From first-class dive school, I was stationed on the Island of Guam for three months. What stood out the most about Guam was how humid it was there. In the morning I would walk down a hill from our Seabee base to where the dive locker was, and the air was so thick it seemed as though one could cut it with a knife.

The diving was good, not as good as Diego Garcia, but at least Guam had "civilization" and wasn't just military, as on Diego Garcia. Our main diving responsibility on Guam was to help the dive locker at Apra Harbor at the US Naval Base.

On our days off, we had the liberty to dive where we wanted on the island, and we came across a WWII Japanese plane in 50 feet of water. Someone had removed the propeller from it, and the coral was starting to engulf it. Guam saw major battles in WWII, with both the Americans and Japanese forces taking the island.

Saturation Dive School

My heart's desire on Guam was to be accepted to the navy's saturation dive school. But despite having graduated top of my class from all three schools, the navy sent me to— steelworker school, second-class dive school, and first-class dive school, to God be the glory! Yet saturation dive school was not opened to me.

I stood inside of the main dive locker at Apra Harbor at the US Naval Base, proudly wearing my first-class diving pin and talking over the phone to my mom, who was in the States. "Garry, your dad is out and will not be back till later." But she added, "Your dad is sure proud of you, son. He brags about you everywhere he goes."

"Good." I said, because that was the reason I'd joined the navy and become a diver, to make him happy.

Then I shared with my mom how frustrated I was because I could not get the navy to approve my request to be a saturation diver. I was rejected because my job classification as a Seabee was steelworker, and the navy had no openings for this skill in saturation diving. I appealed this, contending that they did have openings for ship fitter, which was basically the same thing, but my request was still denied.

My mom said, "Son, whoever makes this decision will have a secretary, and you should send her a box of chocolates and a big bouquet of flowers. And then ask her to get it approved."

My first thought was, *That's not going to do anything.* But I had no other recourse; there was nothing left for me to try. So I followed my mom's advice, and a week later I received orders for saturation dive school. It was good this worked out, because sometimes I had the impression the cards were stacked against me. *Thanks, Mom, and thank You, Lord, for using her.*

Point Loma, California

I graduated fourth in my class from the navy's saturation dive school, a fourteen-week program, at Point Loma, California. I was not a Navy SEAL—I was a saturation diver trained to live on the ocean floor. Most people assume that if one is a navy diver, then he is a SEAL, but this is not the case. We are all proud of our Navy SEALs, but they are not one and the same as navy saturation divers. Some SEALs have become saturation divers (there were two in my saturation class), but this is not common. Saturation divers are not trained for combat— as are SEALs—but for deep working dives of extended periods of time. We were told there were more SEALs than saturation divers (200 saturation divers in 1975, and I heard figures of 300–400 Navy SEALs).

While at the navy saturation dive school, I made two training saturation dives from the USS *Elk River*, which was originally used as a support vessel for the US Navy SEALAB program. But after the SEALAB program ended with the death of diver Berry Cannon, this ship was used in conjunction with the saturation dive school at Point Loma. These saturation training dives were 190 feet for three days. Being divided up with one day at depth and two days of decompression. We stayed in a diving chamber on the USS *Elk River*, and to make our water entries, we were moved to a personnel transfer capsule that was then lowered through an open well in the center of the ship. While at 190 feet we were in the ocean for a couple of hours. This was by San Clemente Island just off the Southern California coast.

Upon graduation from saturation dive school us divers received an increase in or base pay. They told us that saturation divers received the highest professional pay (ProPay) in the US Navy. Saturation divers from this school went to either the Navy Experimental Diving Unit (NEDU) in Panama City, Florida, or to two ASR 21 class of submarine rescue ships.

Whispers of Something Secret

I thought, *I have arrived! I have gone as far as anyone can in the field of diving.* But I was wrong.

During my time at saturation dive school, in the evening when I was at our barracks, I had heard the word "projects," and another time "special projects" come up in conversation. And both times it was from a group of SAT (saturation) divers assigned to the nuclear submarine the USS *Halibut,* which had docked at Point Loma.

I asked a SAT diver, "What were you divers talking about when you mentioned the 'projects'?" He was visibly afraid and walked away without saying a word. The next time I asked another SAT diver, he responded, "You need to ask someone else." This only made me more curious, and I asked a diver friend who had been in the navy longer than I, and he said, "It's the secret stuff the navy does, and to know more you will have to be cleared for it."

Surprisingly, upon graduation from SAT school, I received orders to the "projects," even though I had applied for the Navy Experimental Diving Unit. Looking back now, I believed God had His hand in this and was working in my life. However I was not sent directly to the USS *Halibut*. Instead I went to a support barge for special projects, at Point Loma. I signed a nondisclosure agreement and was on this barge for several months, and bit by bit things were revealed. That's when I realized why the government had spent so much money training us for saturation diving, "secret stuff."

More Than Defense

During the Cold War most everything the military did was for defensive purposes. Being prepared for something you hope never happens—war. This is not in vain, as an adversary is far less likely to attack you if he knows you have the capabilities to respond. But this project was not defense but offense. Going to the enemy's territory to get something of value for the USA. They needed saturation divers for this, and I wanted to be in on it. I liked the espionage part, but mainly because it was by all measures something important.

Chapter V
Soviet Embassy, Washington, D.C.

CIA Release

"Mired in debt, Pelton declared bankruptcy … Called the Soviet embassy in Washington and asked if he could come by. Although that call was intercepted by the FBI (tapes of the two conversations were played at the trial last week), the bureau at the time did not or could not identify Pelton and intercept him." (Declassified in Part—Sanitized Copy Approved for Release 2012/02/24: CIA-RDP90-00965R000402680002-3)

FBI

Two blocks from the Soviet Embassy, three FBI agents are in a van eavesdropping on their phone lines. Then they hear Ronald Pelton's voice on the phone.

The chief agent says, "Hey, guys, this is him. Get a trace on his line."

Pelton is arguing on the phone about payment. "I told you I have something you will want to know about, but I need help now, not sometime in the future."

The Russian says, "Yes, of course, but you know this is a two-way street. You have your concerns, and we have ours."

Pelton butts in, "You didn't check on my credentials?"

The Russian responds, "Yes, yes, we will need to discuss this more, but not over the phone!" And then Pelton is told to meet with them at a prearranged location.

But Pelton raises his voice. "What about the payment? I have creditors!"

"Of course, and we want to help, but we need to talk about this face to face."

Pelton hangs up.

The FBI agent asks, "Have you got this traced?"

"It's from a nearby phone booth."

"Go see if he is still there. We want this guy!"

The Washington Metro

Pelton enters a subway car and sees his contact. They both glance around. Pelton is nervous and argumentative about being paid. The Russian says, "We told you not to call us at the embassy. In fact, it would be better if you visited our country, where you would be treated hospitably, and of course, with all the comforts."

"No!" responds Pelton. "I want money! What is it with you people? What aren't you getting?"

The Soviet responds, "If you do not feel comfortable with meeting us in Mother Russia, then you must understand there are concerns we have. And these sort of things works better in a foreign country. How about Europe? Say, Vienna?"

"Sure, I will go on a vacation to Vienna. Just give me the money!"

"We will call you at the place and time we talked over before. But don't call us again at the embassy!"

Chapter VI
Mare Island Naval Shipyard
Bay Area, California

In 1974 I received orders to the nuclear-powered submarine the USS *Halibut* SSN-587. Her name, *Halibut*, a somewhat bland name for a nuclear submarine, came from the unusual looking sea fish halibut, also called a flat fish. Unlike other fish that continuously swim, the halibut spends most of its time lying on the ocean floor. Similarly, the USS *Halibut* also had an unusual look and often would sit on the ocean floor during her special operations, sometimes for as long as two months, not counting transit time to and from the project.

Love at First Sight

The USS *Halibut* was tied up at dock, she was 350 feet long, made of HY-80 steel (able to withstand 80,000 pounds psi), was painted all black, and the American flag fluttered from her stern. The guard on the *Halibut* had a .45 caliber sidearm and registered all who came aboard. I was standing on the dock with two other saturation divers, smiling and looking at the USS *Halibut*.

"Matheny, what do you think of the *Halibut*?" asked Rich, one of the divers.

"As a child, I saw the Disney film *20,000 Leagues Under the Sea*, and ever since, I've been fascinated by the mystique of submarines. To me this is love at first sight."

They laughed. Rich said, "When subs were being assigned to navy captains, our captain, Captain Larson, did not smile when he was given command of the *Halibut*. Of course, the best captains want the newest and fastest subs, but *Halibut* is slow. Dr. Henry Kissinger was said to have been in the room when Captain Larson received his orders. And Dr. Kissinger took him to the side and told him enough about the *Halibut* and her mission that it put a smile on his face."

Tom, the other diver, said, "Matheny, here comes the COB. He probably wants to assign you your bunk."

COB (Chief of the Boat), was the highest noncommissioned officer on the submarine. He was fiftyish and full of Irish wit. He said, "You must be the new diver, Matheny. Follow me."

COB and I, after signing aboard, went down through the hatch and narrow ladder into the sub. We immediately enter the area where the periscopes were. The duty officer was sitting on a chair and looking at us, and there were three technicians calibrating equipment.

I was immediately struck with how many components were crammed into this space and all the way down the narrow hallway. The entire ceiling was covered with electrical cables and pipes, and the curved walls had more pipes and hundreds of valves and switches. I stood there wondering how anyone could know what they were all for.

"They call this area the CONN," COB said. "It is the main control area of our sub. Follow me down the stairs to the lower level."

The "stairs" were not much more than a narrow ladder at a steep angel. I held on to the railing to keep from falling, but once I was used to them, I could almost run down them. Then we entered a narrow passageway that was lined with bunks on both sides, three bunks high.

"By the way, you will bunk in the aft torpedo room, bunk three," said COB, and then asked, "Where are you from?"

"From the back of beyond. I grew up in the Sierra Nevada Mountains, and my closest neighbor was four miles away."

"I was raised on a farm in Kansas, and there were no kids my age anywhere around me. So I had no one to teach me how to be 'cool,'" said COB, and we both laughed.

As we went through the narrow passageways, I asked COB, "What's that smell? I smelled it the moment I came on board."

"That oily machinery smell is something all subs have. You will get used to it after a couple of days. Lot of things are different here." COB stopped and pointed to a small room and said, "That room is for us chiefs. It is off limits to you."

COB seemed to enjoy talking about the sub. "There will be an orientation in a couple of days for you and two other new sailors. But they are already sub qualified. So for all you landlubbers, I have to bring you up to speed on the living conditions in a boat. And it is proper to call a submarine either a ship, sub, or boat.

"First, the longer you're out to sea, the more you wish you were in port. Yes, one gets bored and homesick. After a long deployment, when you get off the sub, you will notice how tanned everyone else is compared to you. Oh, look to the right. That hole in the wall is our galley [the kitchen on a naval vessel]. Next to it is the chow hall, which is too small for all of us, so we eat in shifts. The chow hall is were we hangout, play cards, or read a book. They show us movies here sometimes. Let's take a seat and have coffee.

"We use the power from our nuclear reactor to produce fresh water by desalinating seawater. Subs also have dehumidifiers to prevent the buildup of humidity that will condense on our steel walls and equipment. We remove all the carbon dioxide we exhale with chemical filters. And we produce our own oxygen by 'burning oxygen candles' (sodium chlorate and iron powder). I know, it sounds strange, but it works.

"Names are given to each group on our sub: 'Bubble-heads' are submariners, 'Nukes' work on the reactor, the 'God Squad' are Christians, 'Spooks' are the NSA cryptologists, and you divers are called 'Riders,' as you are not sub qualified. And you are also called 'Prima Donnas.'"

"Hey! Why do they call us that?"

"Some of you divers think you're special because our sub is a diving platform, it exists for you divers, to bring you to and from the dive location. And you divers are known for getting all upset when you are not picked for a dive."

"And who picks which divers will make the dives?" I asked.

"Glad it's not in my hands," said COB. "Anyhow, on a sub the only way you can tell if it is night or day is by looking at your watch, unless one happens to be by the CONN, when they 'Rig for Red.' The normal lighting is turned off, and red lights come on so that if we need to surface, we can see immediately without the need to adjust our eyes to the darkness.

"Subs have 18-hour days—we sleep six hours, work six hours, and study or relaxed six hours. And it works OK, but the food schedule is on a 24-hour day—every six hours we eat, first breakfast, then lunch, then dinner, and then a snack. However, this does not correspond to how we sleep: when a person wakes up one morning, it will be breakfast, and two days later when he wakes up, it will be dinner.

"In short, submarines are an alien world with no phones, no TVs, no sun, no windows, no women—and no one ever asks you how the weather is. Welcome to the *Halibut*!

COB then put his coffee cup down. "Oh, and Matheny, you are to report to Security."

Chapter VII
Security

"Matheny, what do you think of the mission?" Asked the security officer, who was sitting at a desk in a small room with papers in his hand.

"I think it's smart."

"Really? Take a seat," said the security officer.

"Sure. You know the Russians are trying to get information from us. It would be irresponsible not to do the same."

Security Officer nodded in agreement. "We finished your background investigation, and your top-secret clearance has been approved. I see you have already signed your nondisclosure act.

"You're not to travel to any foreign countries. Nor are you allowed to go into electronic stores, like Radio Shack, because of the possible connection with the operation.

"There are only 30 people on this sub who know what the mission is and where it will be going. While in port all you divers are at the far end of the base in the old World War Two barracks. This way there will be less mixing with others, less chance of inadvertently giving away our operation.

"Your navy service folder that has all of your records will not contain any information about this project or even the name of the project. We do not want those in admin, who handle your records, to read about this operation.

"Our government has sent out teams to try and find out what the mission is. The thought being that if our guys can figure it out, then our enemies could also, and security will need to be beefed up. The navy has planted some sailors among us who will try and get us to talk about the operation. When someone asks you about the project, whether on or off base, you will respond with a simple, 'No comment.'" If anyone pesters you for information about the operation, then give us his name and we will take care it.

Through the Years

For years after I was discharged from the navy, others had asked me what I was doing as a diver on a submarine. When I told them it was still classified, some would take an offense, as though I were personally against them, but if they were in my position, they would have done the same.

Only Three Categories

Sometimes TV programs, books, or films will say something like, "Top Secret or above." But at that time, and as I understand it today also, there are really only three categories: confidential, secret, and top secret. These can, however, be compartmentalized—in other words, top secret for NATO is different from top secret for the US Army or top secret Crypto. And if someone had a top secret clearance for a program he was working on, this would not in itself allow him to view information of another top secret program, except on a need-to-know basis.

Chapter VIII
Sold Out in Vienna, Austria

CIA Release

"To contact Pelton, the Soviets had him wait for a call at the pay phone of a suburban Virginia pizzeria ... the caller directed him to another pay phone, where he picked up $2,000 in a hidden magnetic box and received instruction to travel to Vienna." (Declassified in Part—Sanitized Copy Approved for Release 2012/02/24: CIA-RDP90-00965R000402680002-3)

CIA Release

"The Soviets uncovered the U.S. operation, which involved the use of American submarines, after debriefing Pelton during two extended sessions in Vienna ..." (Declassified

Soviet Embassy

At the Soviet embassy in Vienna, Mr. Pelton meets the man he had talked to in the States. He introduces him to two other men who would do the debriefing and assures him that if all goes well, each day he will be walking out with "proper compensation." In the debriefing room there is a third man, a KGB intelligence officer named Lieutenant Mirgayas Volkov. Pelton is introduced to him, but the KGB officer only nods his head and says nothing during the whole interview. They ask Mr. Pelton many questions about the inner workings of the NSA.

But Pelton becomes frustrated and says, "That's not the important thing. What is really important is where we are getting our information from—we're getting it straight from you!"

The KGB officer, who is in the background, is smoking a cigarette and studying Mr. Pelton. Pelton walks over to a world map and points to a location, saying, "You're losing information to America right here."

CIA Release

"The location that Pelton pointed to on the map was the Sea of Okhotsk between the Kamchatka Peninsula and the eastern Soviet coastline ..." (Declassified and Approved for Release 2011/12/19: CIA-RDP9000965R000706870011-5)

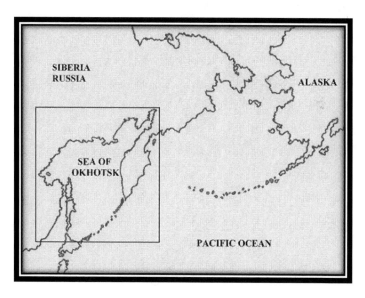

Sea of Okhotsk

Moscow

Mr. Orlov, who is in charge of the KGB security, is in his office when he receives a phone call from Lieutenant Volkov.

"The two men who did the debriefing are still suspicious that Mr. Pelton might be a plant trying to gain our confidence," Lieutenant Volkov says, "But because he checked out as being an NSA cryptologist, I do not see that we have any choice but to follow up on this."

"Well, if you do find anything let me know," says Mr. Orlov, and hangs up.

Chapter IX

Orientation

There was a large drawing of the *Halibut*, and COB briefly explained the different compartments and which ones were off limits. COB pointed to the drawing with a pointer stick. There were three new sailors, including myself.

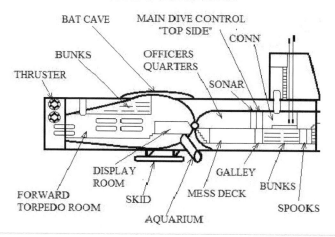

INTERIOR USS *HALIBUT* (SSN-587)

"Gentlemen you are on a one-of-a-kind submarine. No other sub in the world has the unique silhouette of the USS *Halibut*. There is a huge metal bubble on the deck of the sub, named the 'bat cave.' It is the largest door on any submarine that I know of. Designed originally for cruise missiles before she was converted to a special project boat.

"The project officers love this huge door because they can load large items onto our sub without taking them apart. You will learn more about the project officers later, but be advised, they are not the same as the other officers on our sub. Project officers are not involved in the guidance or control of the *Halibut* but are solely for the oversight of the special ops.

INTERIOR USS *HALIBUT* (SSN-587)

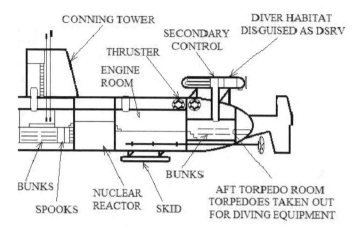

CONNING TOWER

DIVER HABITAT
DISGUISED AS DSRV

SECONDARY
CONTROL

THRUSTER

ENGINE
ROOM

BUNKS

BUNKS
SPOOKS

NUCLEAR
REACTOR

SKID

AFT TORPEDO ROOM
TORPEDOES TAKEN OUT
FOR DIVING EQUIPMENT

"On the tail end of *Halibut* is something that looks like a mini sub, with 'DSRV Simulator' written on its side."

COB smiled as he told us a short story. "One time when we were on the surface and coming into San Francisco Bay, a newscaster who was in a helicopter reported seeing our sub. He described her as looking like she was pregnant"—COB points to the bat cave—"and carrying a baby on her stern, the DSRV Simulator.

"Let's cover some basic facts. The *Halibut* has two levels in the middle section, with the upper level being made up mostly of the officers' quarters and the CONN.

"The *Halibut* also has side thrusters. With these, she can maintain a stationary position while hovering over the ocean floor. And albeit slowly, she can even move sideways! *Halibut* was not overhauled so she would be fast, but to find things. Her capability to maneuver like no other submarine has made her the sub of choice for special projects.

"Next is the aquarium. This is a sea lock for lowering a towed 12-foot-long underwater search vehicle called the 'Fish.' This Fish comes with lights and is equipped with cameras for searching the seafloor. Its purpose is to find 'stuff' in the water.

"Then there is the 'Swimming Eye Ball,' otherwise known as the Eye. This is also let down through the aquarium. Its purpose is to film 'stuff' in the water.

"*Halibut* has four very large skids, for sitting on the ocean floor. Something rare for a submarine. I believe the divers call these skids 'tennis shoes.'

"Now the following areas are off limits! The computer room, display room, NSA room, and the officers' quarters. And only the divers are allowed in the aft torpedo room."

One of the new sailors interrupted. "COB, I'm a torpedoman's mate. I will have to go to the aft torpedo room."

"What for? All the torpedoes have been taken out."

Torpedoman's Mate asked, "Why aren't there torpedoes there?"

COB responded, "If you don't know, don't ask! Don't you just love spy subs?!

Besides, your bunk is in the forward torpedo room, which has plenty of torpedoes."

"Now it's time for chow!"

Chapter X
Saturation Diving

Classroom

Our instructor liked to teach at *full throttle*. "Okay, all you hotshots. I know you think you're lean, mean machines, but if you flunk my class, you don't dive, so listen up!" We wanted to dive and sat up straight in our chairs, giving him our full attention.

The classroom had diving equipment and 20 saturation divers. There were charts, diving rigs, face masks, wet suits, and a three-foot-long section of five cables bundled together. On the wall were diving emblems, an American flag, and signs: "Freedom isn't free—someone paid a price." And "Keep America strong—little old ladies get mugged, not prizefighters."

Our instructor was a qualified saturation diver and knew the new diving equipment on the *Halibut*. He was going over procedures and differences between that of saturation dive school and the system on our sub.

"Today we will be going over our Westinghouse diving rig, called the Abalone or Mark 11. It comes with all the whistles and bells, all of which will be explained."

He now took the diving rig and held it as though it were a baby. "I know of only six of these dive rigs, so if you drop one of them, it will be the end of your diving career. And you will be lower than whale puke anywhere in special projects! Can I hear a hearty 'Yes, sir!'"

A chorus of "Yes, sir!" rang out.

"You have all been through three navy diving schools by now, however, *Halibut*'s system is like none other."

He held up a section of a diver's cable. "Attached to each diver are five hoses and wires in a cable that is 350 feet long. It's true you're not able to swim around freely, as in scuba, because we have you on a leash with all these cables connected to you. But by now the average diver in this room has made more than 200 scuba dives and 100 umbilical cord dives. And at a depth of 400 feet, if a diver's blood stream is saturated with mixed gas, even if he was to swim only halfway to the surface, he would die! The truth is, at the site of the dives the visibility is so poor that without your umbilical cable you could easily get lost and not find you way back to the *Halibut.*

"The heliox will be supplied to you through these two hoses, called the push-pull system. One hose will push the mixed gas to you and one will pull it back. So no bubbles will go into the water and reach the surface, and 'Ivan' will not know you are there.

"Then there is the hot-water hose. Remember, that in Siberia you will be diving in 27-degree Fahrenheit water. It would be frozen solid if it was not salt water. You will be wearing two wet suits, the thin liner one-eighth-inch thick, and the outer suit three-eighths-inch thick, with hot water pumped between the two to prevent hypothermia. The hot-water hose will supply you with 140-degree water, which is why you need the inside liner, so as not to be scalded."

Memories of Frigid Waters

On the mission, when we were at the dive station, I put my hand into the seawater just to see how cold it felt, and I could not hold my hand in it. The salt water tried to freeze the blood in my hand, and I could feel it go up my arm and into my heart.

On one of the saturation dives, some gas leaked under my face mask, which was attached to the one-eighth-inch neoprene liner. The gas seeped over my head and was trapped under the liner, causing my face mask to rise up on my face.

On my next saturation dive, I didn't want to fight with my face mask again, so I had this "bright" idea to cut two small holes in the thin liner so any bubbles could go through it and not cause my mask to rise up. The problem was, I didn't realize it would take time for the hot water to circulate up that high in my wet suit. So when I entered the sea, in came the *freezing cold water* straight to my head. It felt like someone was driving two spikes into my brain. I wasn't sure what to do, and when those in diver control kept asking through our communication system why I was not moving out, I stalled for time. A diver just didn't bail out and crawl back into the dive chamber; he might not be allowed to make the dive, as another diver could take his place. Fortunately, after a minute and a terrible headache, the hot water circulated up to my head, and I was able to make the dive.

Classroom

Diver asked, "If for some reason we were to lose our hot water, would the one-eighth-inch liner be enough to get us back in the freezing water?"

"Not alive. The problem is, you will not know you have lost your hot water till you start freezing. In the event of an emergency, say you lose your hot water or get the wrong gas mixture and pass out, your umbilical has a one-quarter-inch wire cable so we can pull you back."

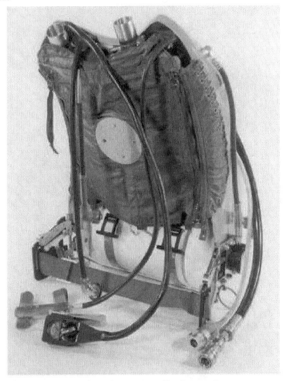

Westinghouse diving rigs.
Courtesy of Gary Lynn

Why We Could Not Use Scuba

Breathing air in a dive of 400 feet would make one dangerously drunk (called *nitrogen narcosis*)—a person would black out at that depth, not to mention the problems with decompression. And breathing pure oxygen at that depth is deadly (called *oxygen toxicity*). So because we could not breathe either air or pure oxygen at 400 feet, we used a special mix of helium and oxygen.

Decompression is when the built-up helium in the bloodstream is given time to come out, so bubbles will not form in the diver's blood. At 400 feet, the pressure on one's body is 12 times (or 12 atmospheres) greater than on the surface. The inside of a submarine is kept at one atmosphere (what we have on the surface), so if a door were opened to the sea at a depth of 400 feet, including a door on the bottom of a submarine, the seawater would rush in faster than any fire hydrant and flood the sub. However, our diving chamber was kept at the same pressure as the outside water—in our case 12 times greater than on the surface—and the room from which we entered the water was open to the sea on the bottom part of it. But the water did not come in because this room was pressurized.

This extra pressure in our diving chamber meant divers were breathing 12 times as much gas in one breath as they would on the surface. All this "extra" gas went into our lungs and was forced into our bloodstream. When a soda bottle is opened, the fizz comes from the carbon dioxide bubbles that come out of the soft drink. But if a soda bottle is opened very slowly, then no fizz is heard and no bubbles are seen coming out of the liquid. Similarly, we decompressed slowly, letting the pressure off to give time for the gas to come out of our bloodstream.

The "bends" is another major concern in saturation diving. Bends is when the tiny helium bubbles (or nitrogen from air) come out of a diver's blood and block arteries or veins in his joints, lungs, or brain. Even when following the decompression tables, not everyone's metabolism can handle this.

The bends can be treated either by pressing a diver back down again (recompression) so that any bubbles will go back into his bloodstream, or by having him breathe a different gas to help in the exchange rate of the built-up gas in his blood. But this is not an exact science, and if the damage is too great, no amount of treatment will help.

One of the saturation divers from our team was bent (had the bends), but he completely recovered. But I knew of other navy saturation divers who were bent and they did not completely recover.

It is called saturation diving because in a dive of more than 12 hours, the bloodstream becomes saturated with whatever gases (in our case helium and oxygen) a diver breathes, and he cannot take any more into his bloodstream unless he goes deeper.

Donald Duck

Our Instructor continues, "Also, you have your communication cable. This face mask has a headset and speaker for communications, which is connected to the helium speech descrambler in the dive chamber. You will need this because the helium will make you sound like Donald Duck—an effect brought on by the helium on your vocal cords.

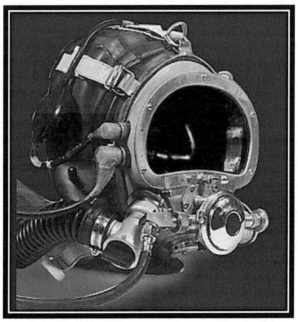

Modified Kirby Morgan band mask
Courtesy of H I Sutton, Covert Shores.

"Your face mask is doubled sealed, one seal around your face and one around your mouth and nose, so if the face mask gets flooded, you can still breathe.

"Your diving rigs are semi-rebreathers, which means you rebreathe your mixed gas. Only one in six breaths will be a fresh supply of gas. This rig will scrub the carbon dioxide that you exhale, and the fresh gas mix will be supplied by your hoses. Our semi-rebreather also heats the mixed gas you breathe, as the freezing water makes the gas so cold it will give you a headache. This is even a bigger problem with helium because of its poor thermal properties, which takes heat away from your body.

"There are pockets in this outer wet suit for your weights. Keep your buoyancy slightly negative. Also, each diver has a flashlight and two knives. One is the standard issue K-bar knife with an eight-inch blade, plus this smaller knife with a one-inch sharp blade." (For a diver, a knife is basically a tool.)

Our instructor held up a one-foot-long, four-inch-wide metal cylinder. "Listen up, what I have here is your come-home bottle for emergency return. It is filled with a premixed heliox gas for the depth of your dives. In the event of an emergency and your gas supply is cut off, this come-home bottle will automatically start releasing gas into your dive rig. It is actuated by a small sensor when the pressure of the mixed gas falls off. At 400 feet, this emergency bottle would only last a few breaths. But because your dive rig is a semi-rebreather, it should last long enough to get you back to your dive chamber.

"In the event your mixed gas somehow gets blocked, you will know this by a red light that will come on. This red light is on the inside of your face mask. If this comes on, you immediately return to your dive chamber and inform diver control that you have a red light."

Master Diver

The diving officer and master diver came in and asked for a word with us. The master diver spoke first. He was a sharp guy, not braggadocios, and knew the entire system. We trusted him.

"Regardless of the fact that you have all made saturation dives before, no one will be picked who has not made a saturation dive from the *Halibut*. On a previous training saturation dive on the *Halibut*, a diver who was saturation qualified became scared at depth, froze up, and had to be brought back in.

Obviously, we are not going to experiment on location to find out who can and who cannot do this. Also, most of you have only made saturation dives to 190 feet for three days, but these practice dives will be to 420 feet for seven days. All this will prepare you and give you confidence for the actual mission."

Only Eight Divers Would Be Chosen

The diving officer spoke next. "Guys we are scheduled to have two saturation dives at the site. And only eight of you will make the dives and enter the water.

"I know most of you want to make these dives and we will be evaluating each of you to determine who will be chosen. But all of you will be necessary to man the two control stations, which will run nonstop during the dives. So, do your best and have a team spirit."

One diver asked, "When will we know who the eight of us are that will be making these dives?"

"We will let you know after we leave port for the mission, when we are two weeks out to sea. You're dismissed."

Chapter XI
Briefings

The briefings were about our project, what we were doing, why we were doing it, the risks involved, and security. These briefings were sometimes informal and sometimes tense, about high stakes. We had some briefings on the sub and a couple in an auxiliary building at Mare Island.

During one briefing, a skipper explained how at a luncheon, a reporter came up to some submarine captains and asked them questions about their missions. One of the captains responded, "And what flavor of ice cream do you like?" Then the reporter asked the skipper a question he knew was ridiculous and received the response he deserved, but was actually hoping for. The captain told him, "That's absurd!" But the reporter followed up with, "I understand you are carrying out covert operations." Whereupon the captain became silent. The next day the newspaper headline was, "Sub Captain Denied Some Missions, But Not Covert Operations."

Admiral on deck!

There were 30 men crammed into a small room, most sitting on the floor, waiting for an admiral.

An officer hollered out, "Admiral on deck!"

All in the room stand and snap to attention.

Admiral Thompson entered and said, "At ease. Find someplace to sit on the floor. My apologies about the room, but security thought it best we meet in a room with no windows.

"Everyone in this room has had the necessary background checks, you have all signed your nondisclosure acts, and everyone here has a top-secret clearance. Look around you. Out of 130 men on the *Halibut*, only the divers, these officers, and two NSA analysts will know what the mission is, where we are going, and what we are doing. Even some of the officers on the *Halibut* do not know the mission.

"I don't need to tell you how important it is that we do not let slip what we are doing. 'Loose lips sink ships.' Under the wrong set of circumstances, this is the sort of thing that could start World War III, but it is also the sort of thing that could help end the Cold War."

Admiral Thompson walked over to a map and pointed to the sea of Okhotsk. "You are being sent out on a three-month mission. You are going to the Sea of Okhotsk, which the Soviets claim as their territorial waters. The Russians have an underwater military cable there, and we are going to tap it! Obviously, the more we know of their operations, the less of a threat the Russians are to us, and lack of intel makes us vulnerable. We do not want another Pearl Harbor.

"*Halibut* will be entering in through the Kuril Islands. This is one place we are certain that the Russians have an underwater acoustic range listening for foreign submarines. But our subs are quieter than theirs, and we have done this before and we can do it again.

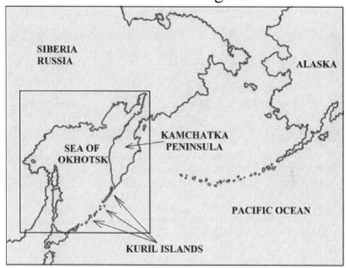

"We all know that the *Halibut* is not fast, but no sub would be if it had to push through the water giant skids and a fake DSRV. *Halibut* was chosen for her maneuverability, not her speed. Besides, at the point of entry, there will be a friend waiting for you, she is faster than anything the Russians have, and she will watch out for you.

"As you know, to have even one saturation diver on a submarine is unheard of, but 20 saturation divers is a very large red flag.

Therefore, a plausible cover story has been created. The Soviets are presently testing their cruise missiles and have a splash zone in this same sea. The story will be spread that you are going there to try and recover what is left over from these missiles. You will not need to circulate this story—we will. And when asked about it, only give our standard 'No comment.'

"A word to you divers—every diver who gets in the water will be put in for the Legion of Merit. It is one of the highest medals our nation gives without being in combat."

Chapter XII
National Security

When the operation faced exposure because of Ronald Pelton's trial, both former president Ronald Reagan and CIA Director William Casey tried to stop the leaks.

CIA Release

"But Casey has gone public in recent weeks with strong criticism of the press ... one of NSA's most sensitive secrets, a project with the code name Ivy Bells, believed to be a top-secret underwater eavesdropping operation by American submarines inside Russian harbors." (Declassified and Approved for Release 2012/09/25: CIA-RDP90-00965R000302100006-3)

CIA Release

"President Reagan personally telephoned *Washington Post* Chairman Katharine Graham to ask that her newspaper not print an article on

'Ivy Bells,' the U.S. eavesdropping operation in Soviet harbors ... " (Declassified and Approved for Release 2012/02/28: CIA-RDP90-009658000504130034-5)

"Your wife has been sending codes."

When we were out to sea, wives would send family grams to their husbands. Those who were Christians would sometimes receive a Bible verse from their wives. These family grams were limited in length, and in order to get as much in as possible, a wife would sometimes send a Bible reference and not spell out the verse. Then her husband could look it up in his Bible. This got the attention of security, who feared that these were some sort of code, and they wanted to know "Who is John 3:16?"

The Government Was Serious!

I heard that our security got to the point that those saturation divers (or anyone) who asked about this project, in the hopes of coming to it, were not accepted. The thought being that if we were ever infiltrated, it would be by a spy who would ask to join us.

While on the *Halibut* and out to sea on our 1975 deployment, one of the Nukes decided to write a book about our mission. Of course, the mission was still classified at that time. Had his book gotten out into the open, it would have been either the end of the operation, or at the least, put in danger the sailors on the other submarines that took *Halibut*'s place. It was purposely leaked that he was mistaken about our mission, which he was. Most of the crew did not know what our mission was, and this sailor was not privy to this information.

This sailor's book was found, and he suffered the consequences: for the rest of the mission, he was confined to his bunk and had his food brought to him.

Leaving port with loved ones standing on the pier sad or crying, is hard. Many sailors say their goodbyes at home as it is easier to deal with. But when you come home after a long deployment and see your family and loved ones waiting on the pier and waving to you, it is one of the greatest feelings. Everyone on our sub looked forward to this, and we all had smiles. Except for one Nuke.

The *Halibut* had radioed security about the situation shortly before we made port. I had forgot about him because he had been restricted to his bunk, and I had not seen him again until the day we got back to port at Mare Island. His wife met him at the dock, and they walked away from the rest of us. She was very upset about something, and he became visibly despondent with the news she shared. I found out a week later that the government had searched his home while we were still out to sea, and I was told that this was just the beginning of his problems. And this sailor didn't even know what the mission was.

Ronald Pelton

Our government was not going to play around with security, nor should they, it was *our* national security that was at stake. Ronald Pelton, the man who betrayed our operation, was later tried and convicted of espionage and sentenced to three concurrent life sentences at the Federal Correctional Institution of

Allenwood, Pennsylvania. After thirty years in prison he was released and is presently under house arrest.

Chapter XIII
Vladivostok, Siberia

CIA Release

Spy satellites can take pictures of the earth's surface and have the ability to record radio signals, but top-secret information is sent through cables.

"Also reported was the tapping into undersea cables on the Soviet coast, along which the Russians sent military traffic too sensitive to entrust to the airwaves." (Declassified and Approved for Release 2012/02/03: CIA-RDP91-00561R000100120051-2)

CIA Release

"Pelton case: He told the jury about the NSA's ability to exploit, process and analyze coded Soviet communications ..." (Declassified in Part—Sanitized Copy Approved for Release 2012/01/25: CIA-RDP90-00965R000201370001-1lq)

Our NSA analysts, with their computer-deciphering capabilities, could decipher even what was encrypted.

Soviet Naval Base

KGB officer Lieutenant Mirgayas Volkov, who was at the Vienna debriefings with Mr. Pelton, goes to Siberia seeking answers, trying to verify Mr. Pelton's story. Volkov meets Admiral Anatoly Gorshkov in his large office overlooking their naval fleet at Anchorage.

"Welcome to Siberia, Lieutenant Mirgayas Volkov," says Admiral Gorshkov, the 63-year-old commander of the Soviet Pacific Fleet. "Lieutenant Volkov, isn't it a clear, beautiful day?" says the admiral as he sips his coffee spiked with vodka.

"Well, I thought it a little windy," Volkov says.

"Windy, perhaps."

The admiral's voice raises as he says, "I was told by Moscow you were coming out here. Something about Americans spying on us, on one of our underwater cables." As he says this, he walks over to a large map on the wall of his office, which includes the Sea of Okhotsk.

Admiral Gorshkov stands in front of the map without pointing to anything and turns toward Volkov. "And I understand you did not get this information from one of our spies but from a man who sold out his country."

"Well, yes," Volkov says.

"And you believe him?"

"I have no choice but to make sure. It is possible the Americans may have figured out a way to listen to our phone conversations between our eastern military bases and Moscow."

Admiral Gorshkov turns back toward the map and then asks, "And where on this map did the American say they have penetrated?"

Volkov points to the Sea of Okhotsk.

"Yes, but where in this sea?"

"Admiral, don't you know if we have a cable in this sea?"

"Of course I know! But does the American know?"

"He did not give us anything more specific than this. He is an analyst, not a naval officer. I know we have an underwater military cable in this sea. Admiral I must ask, are all communications sent through this cable encrypted?"

"And why should we encrypt some phone call from a peasant mother who scolds her sailor son for not calling home more often?" Admiral Gorshkov responds.

"But, Admiral—"

The admiral cuts him off. "Yes, there is more than that going through the cable, and yes, some of it is encrypted."

"Admiral, what percentage of our classified transmissions though this cable is encrypted?"

"OK, not much. It takes time and money to encrypt message traffic. Besides, I don't see this being the problem you believe it to be. I did some calling before you came, and those I talked to said it was not possible to tap our underwater cable without shorting it out. And I know it is not easy for anyone to come into the Sea of Okhotsk without us knowing about it. Look at these islands." He points on the map to the Kuril Islands. "This is the only way into and out of this sea, and these islands are ours, and we have an underwater acoustic range here. Its only purpose is to listen for submarines entering this sea, and it is manned 24 hours a day. The moment a sub enters here, they notify us, and we check our records and confirm if it is one of ours or not."

"So have any foreign submarines come through these islands?"

"No! And what is more, our acoustic range has only missed one of our subs coming through in more than a year." Admiral Gorshkov stares at Volkov and says, "I can tell by that look on your face that you are thinking that if one of ours made it through, then perhaps the Americans could also."

"Admiral, I am only trying to verify the story that the American gave to us. If an American sub entered in through the Kuril Islands, she would be long gone before a destroyer came. It makes sense to have a destroyer ready in that area. Plus, a destroyer would have active sonar, something our underwater acoustic range would not have."

Irritated, the admiral says, "One month out of the year, we station a destroyer at the main point of entry into this sea. It is the most probable channel for a foreign submarine to attempt to enter. There is heavy ship traffic in the sea lane between the islands there, and a sub who wants to enter undetected will try to mask its noise by following under a freighter or oil tanker. A destroyer is due to be stationed there starting next week. I will inform her captain of your concerns." Admiral Gorshkov laughs. "The captain of this destroyer is new, a Lieutenant Nikolay. He wants to make a name for himself. But at least he will be vigilant."

Lieutenant Volkov insists, "But, Admiral, there are many channels here, and you only want to keep one destroyer there, and that for only a month?"

"Yes, you're right. There are many islands here, and most of these channels are deep enough for a submarine to enter through. So were you expecting me to give you half a dozen destroyers? And for how long? And by whose word—a traitor's? I am telling you, neither the Americans nor anyone else can get into this sea without our knowledge, and even if they could, they would not be able to tap our cable."

"Now, Lieutenant Mirgayas Volkov, would you like a drink?"

"I'm sorry, but I have to go. Just one more question, Admiral. If the Americans did come into our sea, could you bring them to the surface?"

"With depth charges, I could bring them to the surface, but why bring them up? It is easier just to torpedo them. These are in Soviet territorial waters. They should not be here!"

What Would Russia do?

In 1960 American pilot Gary Powers had his U-2 spy plane shot down while flying a CIA reconnaissance mission in the Soviet Union airspace. We could expect no less in their territorial waters.

John Pina Craven (chief scientist of the Navy Special Projects Office) said, "Problems pale beside the importance and ultimate impact of the intelligence operations that *Halibut* would be involved in and the grave dangers she would face" (*The Silent War: The Cold War Battle Beneath the Sea*, p. 142).

CIA Release

"Pelton acknowledged that he had admitted to FBI agents ... that his disclosures might have placed in jeopardy 'a few men who needed to go to and from' the project." (Declassified in Part—Sanitized Copy Approved for Release 2012/02/24: CIA-RDP90-00965R000403270006-3)

Scuttle the USS *Halibut*?

Because the *Halibut* was pushing through the water many things that had been added on to it, it was slow and almost anything the Russians had could outrun her. If the Russians knew we were there, the odds were in their favor that we would not get away. There were codes and other secrets on our sub, not to mention the latest technology, and the last thing the navy wanted was for all this to fall into the hands of the Russians. Therefore it was necessary for our sub to have destructive charges to scuttle her in the event the Soviets tried to bring us to the surface.

These were locked in safes in two locations. One was in the aft torpedo room by the bulkhead next to the engine room, and the other was in the forward part of the sub in the lower level by another bulkhead. We were told these were each 50 pounds of TNT, which would have done the job had it been necessary. The Sea of Okhotsk has deep water close to where we dove; therefore *Halibut* could have been sunk in water too deep to have been salvaged.

It was never explained how such a scenario would have been carried out, at least not while I was on board. I suppose COB or one of the officers would have set a timer on the explosives. I also believe they would have done it.

There were life preservers on the *Halibut*, but no rubber life rafts, at least not that I saw. If our sub was forced to the surface, a sailor without a life raft would die within a minute in the freezing waters. If a Russian vessel would have taken us off the *Halibut*, not only would we have been put in prison, but they would have boarded our sub seeking to stop us from sinking her.

If *Halibut* became trapped by the Russians, she would have been scuttled, and I cannot see any likely scenario in which we would have made it off. But then none of us had been forced to be on the Halibut in the first place— we were all volunteers.

Prior to Operation Ivy Bells, when a spy reported back with information on an enemy project, most often there was no way to verify it. But this mission provided us with the conversations of Russian admirals and generals themselves, and that on a daily basis. This definitely grabbed the attention of our intelligence agencies. To hear Moscow, year after year, discussing war plans with the strengths and weaknesses of their equipment and troops was just too great an enticement to pass up. Were there dangers? Yes, but the importance of this mission overshadowed the dangers.

According to the History Channel documentary *Blind Man's Bluff* (produced by A&E Networks with Will Lyman and Sherry Sontag), "Ivy Bells remained the most dangerous operation of the Cold War. Every cable-tapping mission required personal approval of the president."

If I were still young and able to do it again, *I would!* It's dangerous just driving a car. I would not want to do the dangerous things that those in war do—walking around land mines and having bullets whiz past their heads. The truth is, no one on the *Halibut* was afraid, and if they were, they did a good job of hiding it. All one had to say was, "This sub gives me claustrophobia," and he was off the *Halibut*.

The older divers had experienced some close calls and were a little wiser about the concerns of saturation diving. I noticed they were not so eager to make saturation dives. But the only concern we younger divers had was not being picked to make the dives.

Chapter XIV
Don't Disappoint Us!

We were summoned to another briefing shortly before we left port for our project. I wondered why they were doing this now, as we all knew what to expect on the mission. The officer who stood before us said he would introduce us to Commander Wilson. It was explained that the commander would not be in uniform because he was the navy liaison between us, the CIA, and the NSA. We were told to give him our full and undivided attention.

Then Commander Wilson came in wearing a suit and tie, and looked worried. He seemed pressured by higher-ups in the CIA, as though he had been told he will lose his job if we don't get results. He said some things that were funny and some that make us sober.

"Good day," said Commander Wilson.

All in the room responded, "Good day, sir!"

"Our intelligence community keeps using words like 'the intelligence gold mine,' 'pure juice,' and 'the mother lode.' In short, it is the best thing we have ever had. It's invaluable to us! But there is a problem. It lacks two-way communications. Last year on *Halibut*'s second deployment, though there were no dives and no recordings. What she found, the amplifier, was the most important piece to the puzzle. We must have two-way communications, and without this amplifier, with the mode we are using, it is simply not possible.

"Gentlemen, if you walked into a room, unawares to your girlfriend, and overheard her saying on the phone, 'I love you too. And I can't wait to see you and have you hold me,' you'd get upset. But when she turns around and sees you standing there in the room and says, 'Oh, dear, please say hi to *my mom*,' you would have different feeling about it. Well, we don't have this advantage. There are too many things that we do not understand in these communications because we are only getting one side of a conversation. We are doing a lot of guessing, and sometimes it's wrong. Our analysts tell us it would be five times more valuable to them if they knew who was on the other end of these communications and what they were saying."

Commander Wilson then said, "Every project has its problems to solve. And we are sending you there to solve problems, not to come back with excuses. You fix it. You solve it. You make it work!"

Commander Wilson momentarily pauses. "And we know you will come through for us and bring back what we want. *Won't you?!*" The commander looked as though he had been pressured to get this point across, and he looks at each one of us.

A few said, "Aye, sir," and then more say it, and then all of us.

"Good! We want peace, we want to negotiate with the Russians, but we don't want to give away the barn. To have peace treaties and strategic arms negotiations with the Soviets, we need to know what they have. Not what they tell us they have, but what they really have.

"Have you ever played poker with someone? You would have the obvious advantage if you knew what the other guy was holding in his hand. He couldn't bluff you! When our arms negotiators face off with the Russians, we want our guys to have the best and most up-to-date information. Imagine it—we could ask the Russians to give up systems that even their negotiators don't know they have, and then they would have to call Moscow to find out what we are talking about. And if the Russians want to trade off some missile system we know doesn't work, then our guys can tell them, 'That's OK. You can keep it—*we don't want it!*'"

This was greeted with cheers and laughter.

(It would not have taken long for the Russians to suspect that we were getting information from them—but not how we were doing it. And they would have been looking for traitors among themselves.)

Chapter XV

USS *Halibut*, En Route to the Sea of Okhotsk

Surfacing at Night

While in the Pacific Ocean, Sonar Room detected an intermittent noise, metal against metal, and they knew the area of our sub it was coming from. They figured it had to be a metal toggle that was not properly secured. These toggles secured the sub to a pier when in port. In order to enter the Sea of Okhotsk, we needed to get through the Kuril Islands undetected, which we would not be able to do if making this noise.

Nuclear submarines remain submerged during their entire deployment. A submarine's greatest advantage over other ships is its stealth. In all the time I was assigned to the *Halibut*, this was the only time I remember her surfacing while out in the ocean.

It was night, and there was a cloud cover, so satellites could not see us. I was fortunate to have been picked for a three-man team to go topside for a night surfacing of our sub. The other two were a lieutenant who was in charge and a boatswain's mate who was given the job of securing the toggle.

Normally when topside on a submarine underway, there was a harness we wore with a safety line running along the deck. But this did not reach to the area the boatswain's mate needed to get to, leaving him without this safety feature. My job was to cast out a long rope with a life preserver on it so in the event he fell over, he could grab on to it and the sub would not have to circle back and look for him. The boatswain's mate was able to secure the toggle, and no life preserver was needed.

There was a brisk wind that night, but it felt good to breathe the fresh air. Though it was past midnight, the moon still shone through the clouds and lit up the ocean. What impresses me as I looked around in a 360-degree circle, was that as far as I could see in every direction, there was no land, just water. It made me feel insignificant and small compared to the vastness of the ocean. But I did not have long to contemplate the sea's enormity; the task only took a few minutes. And once we were back inside our sub, the outer hatch was closed and *Halibut* dove back under the waves.

The Galley

The galley, where our food was prepared, was incredibly small and almost always busy.

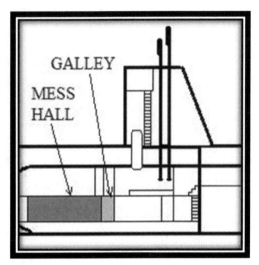

Sailors were waiting in line to get into the chow hall (also called mess hall). A new sailor, named Tom, came in thorough the hatch, holding his head and obviously in pain.

"You OK?" a submariner asked.

"I just found another valve. Am I bleeding?"

We could not help but laugh as he stuck his forehead out for one of us to look at.

"Let me see," said one of the divers, still laughing. "You'll live." And he added, "It took me a week to learn where all the valves were."

"But why do they have to put these valves in the passageways sticking out like that?" Tom asked. "It's not like we have wide passageways." He then went into the "head" (bathrooms on ships) to look in the stainless-steel mirror at his forehead.

A submariner hollered, "Hey, Tom, we are having steak and lobster for dinner."

"Ha-ha" was the new sailor's response.

"It's true," said an NSA analyst. "Once a month they feed us steak and lobster in the same meal. There is no recreation on a sub, so the only morale booster is the food."

Tom stuck his head out from the water closet, holding his forehead, to see if we were serious, and he said, "Well, if that's true, it will be nice, but whoever thought of those powdered eggs needs to be shot."

The cook hollered out, "Make a hole!"

When this was heard, people tried to get out of the way, but it was not always possible. These passageways were, in some cases, not even wide enough to walk down normally, and one had to go through them sideways. Some were lined with bunk beds on both sides. Sometimes a sailor's foot or elbow stuck out into the narrow passageway. And when someone wanted to get around you in a passageway, you were shoved and pushed into a wall.

Three-Bunks High

There is, however, advantages to submarines: They serve the best food and our sub was the only place in the navy I had been where they brought the food to you. One may have to wait in line to get into the chow hall and be seated, but there is no waiting in line for the food. There is so little room to stand in that your food is brought to you.

Chow Hall

Submariners had entered the chow hall and were sitting down at their tables.

Tom asked, "Hey, Spook. Why is your room off limits to us?"

NSA analyst said, grinning, "It's classified!"

"Hmm," said the new sailor.

A submariner entered the chow hall and hollered out, "Everyone has to get their film badge checked today. Be sure and see Doc."

"What?" asked the new sailor.

"That is the little badge they make us wear on our belts. It checks the dosage of radiation we receive from the reactor." explained a submariner.

Radio Man entered the chow hall and hollered, "Family grams for Robert Thompson and Tom Bentley."

Tom Bentley, the new sailor, scrambled out from his seat to grab his family gram. But then he asked, "Where is the rest of my gram?"

Radio Man said, "These family grams are limited to 25 words and only one a week."

"But I can respond back, right?"

Radio Man laughed, "Sure, when we get back in port in three months!" (Though we could receive satellite and radio transmissions, we could not send out any signal or we risked giving away our position.)

NSA analyst asked, "Tom, is that letter from your girl?"

"Yes!" Tom said smiling.

"You going to share that with us?" asked the NSA analyst.

"Sorry guys, it's classified!"

Chapter XVI
Encouragement from Christians

I was a weak Christian, needing encouragement just to show up at the Bible study. I was not trusting God with my decisions and was too concerned about what other people thought. Thankfully, God had His faithful witnesses on our sub, who were more concerned about the Lord.

The first time I went to a prayer meeting, I was sitting at a table in the chow hall, Chief came up to me and tapped me on the shoulder. "A few of us want to meet for prayer at 1800 on the forward port side below the torpedo room. Hope to see you there, and bring your Bible." I nodded my head, but I was such a weak Christian, I did not want others to see me go. Still, when the time came, I make my way forward through the narrow passageways and up to a hatch doorway that I needed to get through. But it was blocked by two sailors.

On the sub (before all the electronic games), entertainment was mostly thinking of ways to play practical jokes on someone. And a favorite pastime was to find someone to poke fun at. The two sailors who blocked the hatch doorway wanted to talk. But I was in a hurry and trying to figure out some way to leave without their asking where I was going. But they kept on talking without giving me a chance to speak. I finally caught on that they were doing it intentionally because, somehow, they had figured out where I was going.

"I've got to go," I finally said.

"Well, don't be late for your prayer time!" They got a laugh out of it.

"Yeah, and I will pray for you," I responded as I pulled out my Bible that I had "hid" in my pocket, and then I went to find the prayer group.

There were five men crammed into a small space. I was surprised to see a couple of them there, and no doubt they were surprised to see me. Still, all of us seemed to enjoy the fellowship, and then they shared a few prayer requests. Chief asked for prayer that God would use us to shine for him and reach others for the Lord. One of the submariners asked for special prayer for his daughter and wife.

I could see that for the submariners and divers who were married, being away from their wives and children weighed heavily on them, and I knew they wished to be home with their families. I was single and did not have to endure being away from my family. Now, as a husband and father, I understand better what they were going through. The military is necessary, and though it's not easy for anyone to be out to sea or at a desert outpost for long periods of time, it is hardest on those who are married.

One of the sailors said, "Chief, there is something I was hoping you could help me with. I have always thought that if I become a

Christian, I could not go to war, or spy for my country. What do you think? Doesn't the Bible say we are not to kill?"

Chief said, "Those are certainly good questions. I do know that both Moses and Joshua sent spies into Canaan. Where the Bible says, 'Thou shalt not kill', it is talking about murder. We cannot take the law into our own hands. I am certainly for peace, but if an enemy invades and starts killing and raping, then the main purpose of our government is to protect us. You can find that written in Romans chapter 13.

"The Bible has many heroes, such as Samson killing the Philistines, which he did when 'the Spirit of the LORD came mightily upon him' or David who killed Goliath. There is a passage in Hebrews 11:33–34 that says, 'Who through faith subdued kingdoms … out of weakness were made strong, waxed valiant in fight, turned to flight the armies of the aliens.'"

Christians Helping Christians

There was a man on our sub I called the Preacher, he gave the messages for our Sunday services. Both he and Chief were greatly used of God to encourage me and others. Unlike me, they based all their decisions around the Lord and His Word. And though they had their dreams, they love the Lord more. Their happiness was in pleasing Him, not in getting their way.

The first time I meet Chief was in a work detail on the *Halibut,* and after working with him for only five minutes he asked, "Garry, are you a Christian?"

I had trusted Christ about a year before being assigned to the *Halibut* and said, in almost a whisper, "Yes."

But Chief said out loud, "Praise the Lord!"

I looked around to see who might have heard, wishing he had not advertised it. But he was genuinely happy he had found another Christian.

Chief explained a lot about God and His Word, and I always had questions for him. Of the many pastors I have known and teachers at Bible college that God has used in my life, the two Christians I owe the most to were not in the ministry. One was Chief and the other was the young man on the Seabee bus who had the courage to witness to me.

I admired Chief's faith and vision to reach others. He was good at organizing things like the prayer time, and he formed a weekly Bible study and, later, a Sunday service. I also looked up to him because he was especially good at dealing with anyone who tried to poke fun at him—something I was not good at. If someone tried to make fun of him, he saw the humor in it, laughed, and then turned it around on the one who started it. And that person would run off. One sailor jokingly asked Chief, "Being how you like to preach to us, if someone dies on the *Halibut,* will you do the funeral?"

Chief laughed and said, "Yes, and I'll do yours for free."

Aft Torpedo Room

I asked, "Chief, you said that God was in control. So why could I not play sports when I was a kid? I wanted too, but we lived too far from town to go to practice. Because after practice the school bus did not run. When I asked my mom about it, she said I should just stay after school, then go to practice, and that she would talk my dad into picking me up. Well, at practice they put me in right field because I didn't know what I was doing. No one ever hits a ball out there anyway. You just have to stay awake. Still, it didn't matter to me, because I was playing baseball.

"Now my dad, when he would get upset, would slam the door on his pickup truck. I was standing out in right field when I heard something that sounded familiar. As I turned my head towards this sound, my dad hollered out in front of everybody. '*Garry get over here*'! I didn't say goodbye to the coach or anyone. I just ran over to my dad's truck, and all the way home he was upset. When we arrived home, my dad was still upset, and he went and told my mom what he thought of her idea of him picking me up.

"I walked down the hall to my bedroom and lay down on my bed. I thought, *Other kids get to play sports, why can't I play sports?* I could have been just as good at baseball as those other kids if I could have practiced."

"You upset because you could not play baseball?" Chief asked.

"No. I went out the next day and went fishing and forgot about it. But that's the point—it did not work out as I had thought, as some other things, so why? I'm not upset. I just don't understand why I could not do that."

Chief responded, "I'm not sure, but I do know God does not have to give an account to us. (Job 33:13) And 'all things work together for good to them that love God.'" (Romans 8:28)

"Chief, my motive in asking you is because I want to make this dive. I do not want to be blocked from it like I was from baseball. There is nothing else I have ever wanted to do as much as this. And God is both the one who can let me do it or keep me from doing it. Is this just my pride and I need to accept whatever comes my way?"

"Garry, sometimes we are just not ready for things, or God has a better plan. But it is interesting to me that Joseph in the Bible told his brothers he would rule over them. And they were upset at him for it. Still, it was God who gave Joseph that dream, even if he was prideful about it. God used Joseph's dream to keep him going in the hard times and then used Joseph to help his people. Maybe your desire is from God. Garry, I would ask God why you want to do this."

Chapter XVII

KGB Headquarters, Moscow

Lieutenant Volkov enters the basement section of the KGB headquarters and walks up to a long counter with three staff personnel. Most people in this area are wearing work clothes rather than suits and either receive or place orders for equipment.

One of the ladies at the counter asks, "How may I help you?"

Volkov says, "I understand that a Mr. Khodjakov works in this area."

The lady at the counter points to a room where Mr. Khodjakov's workshop is.

Lieutenant Volkov opens the door, and Mr. Khodjakov, who is sitting at his desk, recognizes him and stands up. He is surprised and somewhat startled that Lieutenant Volkov has come down to the basement to see him. The room has a large desk but is more of a workshop than an office, with charts and short wooden benches with electrical equipment. Lieutenant Volkov introduces himself, and Mr. Khodjakov says, "I have seen you in the cafeteria a few times. Do you not work on the sixth floor?" (The section where spies are debriefed.)

"Yes, that is right. Mr. Khodjakov I need to ask you a few questions about wiretaps. I understand you are an expert on this sort of thing."

"It is my job, but what specifically?"

"Well, for starters, tell me how you tap someone's telephone."

"All one has to do is cut into the wire and splice a wire to a phone line. It is child's play."

"But, Mr. Khodjakov, what about cables? Tapping into a cable."

"Oh," he responds. "Let's sit down. Yes, communication cables can be more difficult because they most often have multiple wires in them with multiple communications, but one can still find what he wants; it just takes longer."

"What about underwater cables?" asks Lieutenant Volkov.

"You mean like transatlantic cables?"

"Yes."

"So you don't want to tap a party boss, but a country?"

Lieutenant Volkov only smiles.

"Well, I have never tried this. My first thought is the salt water would short out the cable the moment you cut into it."

Lieutenant Volkov insists, "But is there any way you know of to tap a cable or wire without cutting into it?"

Mr. Khodjakov pauses and says, "Well, there is such a way; it is called the inductive mode. When a wire, or in this case, cable, gives off, from its electrical current, an electromagnetic field, we can pick this up by another wire that is wrapped around it. But we don't like to use it, because it is harder to hook up and to take off. Requiring several wraps around a cable to get a good readout. And unless this type of tap was right by a repeater, it would not likely get a strong enough signal through the cable to pick it up."

"Very good!" says Lieutenant Volkov. "It is possible, therefore, to do a tap on an underwater cable without cutting into it and shorting it out."

"Yes, but again, only if the taps are by the repeater that amplifies the signal and sends it out, so the signal will be strong enough."

"Thank you, Mr. Khodjakov. You have been most helpful."

Lieutenant Volkov, in a rush, steps out of the room and passes the long countertop and personnel who are taking orders. He doesn't notice Mr. Orlov, the security expert, who is standing at the counter. Mr. Orlov is talking to one of the ladies there about his new promotion making him the fifth inline to be the head of the KGB. But Mr. Orlov's presence there is not a coincidence, and he is not smiling when he sees Lieutenant Volkov leave Mr. Khodjakov's workshop.

Naval Reference Book

Lieutenant Volkov is in his office and has been looking at drawings of the inductive type of wiretaps. He also has a copy of *Jane's Fighting Ships*, a public reference book with pictures of all the different types of warships, including the USS *Halibut*. And Volkov is particularly interested in the DSRV "simulator" on the fantail of the *Halibut*.

Lieutenant Volkov receives a call from the diving office on the Kamchatka Peninsula. "I have found what you asked for. Our cable on the seabed of the Sea of Okhotsk runs for several hundred kilometers. These repeaters you were interested in are on our cable every six kilometers. The cable is eight centimeters in diameter, and the repeaters themselves are three meters long by 30 centimeters wide. These repeaters pick up the signal, amplify it, and send it out to the next repeater and so on, till, through the cable, it reaches the far side of the Sea of Okhotsk."

"But, Lieutenant Volkov, it could not be as you have thought—divers leaving a submarine to tap our cable. For none of these repeaters would be in a suitable depth for divers from a submarine. There are some in shallow water, but too shallow for a submarine to operate in, and the others are too deep for divers."

Volkov asks, "How deep?"

"According to the chart, the first possible one is 125 meters on the seafloor—far too deep for a working dive."

"Look, I am not a diver," says Volkov, "but how deep can our divers go?"

"Not that deep, not on air, not for the hours it would require—it would kill them. And if our divers breathed a mixed gas that would support them, then literally days of decompression in a chamber. The Americans had something like this called SEALAB, but it did not turn out so well for them, with the death of one of their divers. I was under the impression they had ended it.

"Last year I had made a request to Moscow for us to develop such a deep-dive system. But they said unless I could give a practical purpose for one, they would not allocate the money."

Lieutenant Volkov frowns when he hears this and says, "Perhaps the Americans have found a practical purpose for it."

The diving officer responds, "Well, if they have, then can't you just pull the cable up and see if anything is hanging off of it? If this inductive mode is what they are using, they would not be able to take it off quickly."

"I will make a recommendation that we do just that," answers Lieutenant Volkov, and then hangs up.

Chapter
XVIII
First & Secondary Diver Control

On the tail end of *Halibut* was the DSRV simulator, tubular shaped and approximately eight feet in diameter by 50 feet long. The DSRV (Deep Submergence Rescue Vessel) was designed to rescue sailors from downed submarines (though most of the ocean is below the crush depth of submarines). However, our DSRV was not used for submarine rescue but was bolted to the sub and had no motor or propeller. It was labeled a "simulator" to give the impression we were testing it. But its real purpose was to mask our diving chamber, which had been placed inside it.

There were many articles circulated for the public about the DSRV program, but our "simulator" was used as a cover for our saturation diving system on the *Halibut.* I heard that all the money for this special project was siphoned off from the DSRV program.

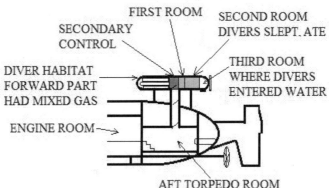

"DSRV SIMULATOR"

FIRST ROOM

SECOND ROOM
DIVERS SLEPT. ATE

SECONDARY
CONTROL

THIRD ROOM
WHERE DIVERS
ENTERED WATER

DIVER HABITAT
FORWARD PART
HAD MIXED GAS

ENGINE ROOM

AFT TORPEDO ROOM

The diving chamber, also called a *habitat* or *hyperbaric chamber*, from which the dives were made, was in the DSRV simulator (hereafter referred to as the DSRV). It was situated directly next to the secondary control room and had space for four divers. We slept, ate, took sponge baths, and made our dives from this small three-room, tube-shaped diving chamber. We could not completely stand up in it because the ceiling was too low. The first room, called the "outer lock," was for "pressing down" more divers or a medical officer in the event of an emergency. The second room, called the "inner lock," was for sleeping and housed a toilet and sink, and the third, called "dive station," was the area from where divers prepared to enter the water. Each compartment of the habitat was separated by round metal doors more than one-inch thick.

The chamber itself was made from aluminum and other metals that would not spark. Even one spark in a chamber under pressure could cause an explosion or, at the least, a fatal fire. All the clothing and other materials inside our habitat, including our towels, were made from an itchy brown fire-resistant material.

Main Diver Control

The saturation dives were manned from two control rooms. Main Diver Control was by the CONN, where the master diver, diving officer, and medical officer monitored the dives. During the dives, we communicated with the Main Diver Control by referring to it as "Topside."

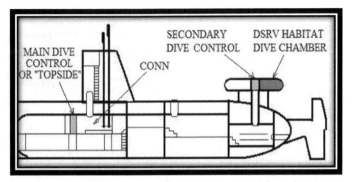

It will be hard for anyone who has not been on a submarine before to imagine just how little space there is. But to add 21 divers, NSA analyst, project officers, plus their food for three months, and then to add display and computer rooms, plus huge mixed-gas cylinders, meant that something had to go. Therefore, the torpedoes had been taken out of the aft torpedo room to make room for our diving equipment.

Secondary Diver Control

The location of the small secondary control room was inside the DSRV (depicted in last drawing), from which we controlled the gas mixtures and depth of the dive chamber (habitat). We entered both the secondary control room and dive chamber by climbing up a ladder from the aft torpedo room.

This control room looked like the inside of a space capsule, and I loved it! It seated two people and contained more than 60 valves, plus pressure gauges for the different gasses, and depth gauges for the pressure inside the different compartments in the habitat. This cramped control room housed about two dozen small lights on a display console that blinked if there was a system failure or problem, such as sudden loss of gas pressure or the need to change a gas supply. In addition, two TV monitors were squeezed into this space, as the navy monitored most everything we did on camera, both inside the diving chamber and, when the diving officer wanted, outside in the water (explained farther down).

It was a lengthy procedure to start up the secondary control room and have it ready for the chamber dives. It took a couple of hours to get it online, requiring several dozen steps that had to be in the right order. The navy did not want this left to our memories. Therefore, we followed a check-off list. One diver would read out loud each setting while the other diver would verify and holler "Check."

We manned this control station nonstop during the dives, pulling four-hour watches. There was a very small window between the diving chamber and this small control room. It was made from Plexiglas and was only three inches in diameter by three inches thick, to withstand the extreme pressures. And besides using the intercom to speak to the divers inside the chamber, you could knock on the metal door to get their attention and then look inside the habitat to see what they were doing.

In addition, there was a small (two-by-one-foot) chamber between the secondary control room and the diver habitat. Those in the secondary control room would use this to convey the food and dishes back and forth to the divers.

One reason I liked this small two-man control room was because it was private. In our sub, there was almost no place you could go where others were not right there by you. And it was the divers' own place; no one else was allowed. When the saturation dives were not going on, I would sometimes go up there just to be alone. You could also spend time with divers and fellowship with them.

There were no personal radios or record players on board the *Halibut,* but someone had brought an eight-track stereo and left it in this small control room. It only had one tape, and the main song was "Yellow Bird, Up High in Banana Tree." (I am laughing out loud while I write this, but that was the song, and the rest of the songs were downhill from there.) And we would play it over and over again, because there was nothing else to listen to. In submarines you are always surrounded by steel, and this song made me think of being on an island someplace with my girl, palm trees, and lots of sunshine. It was the only way to get my mind off the monotony of being underwater for three months.

Chapter XIX
Something Puzzling

At a briefing we were told the navy had found the Soviet cable by searching up and down the shore of the Kamchatka Peninsula, where major Soviet military bases were known to be. They had looked for a sign on the sea coast (through a periscope) that said in Russian, "No mooring in this area!" Because Russia, as all countries that lay cables in the sea, put up such signs where their cables enter the water.

After a briefing about the operation, I met Rich, a diver friend, in the aft torpedo room to play chess.

"Matheny, you been thinking about who is going to be picked? You know, for the dives," Rich asked.

"Yes."

"Hey, it's your move," Rich said.

We talked about our hopes of being chosen to be one of the eight divers, and then he said, "You seem preoccupied."

"I am. There is something. Something I don't understand about that briefing we had today and the cable being *shielded*.* They said the purpose of shielding a cable was so no one could make recordings from it, not even by how we plan to do it. And though this should have stopped us, it doesn't. Are you getting this? Their whole cable is shielded except where we are going to make the taps?

"The story we were told last year was that our guys figured this all out because of what they saw through one of our spy satellites. The Russians brought up their cable because, apparently, it must have had a defect in their amplifier. Anyhow, the Russians replaced it with a new section of cable and a new amplifier. And that even though we knew the rest of the cable was shielded, we waited till they replaced this one section, thinking 'perhaps' the Russians did not bother to shield this section."

"So?" said Rich as he moved a pawn to threaten my rook.

"Well why were we told they found this cable by searching up and down the Russian coast for a sign that read, 'No mooring in this area!' We have both looked through the periscope before and know what you can and cannot see. I help with the charts, and the depths are far too shallow anywhere near the shoreline for our sub to operate and still be able to read a sign on shore."

"If we originally saw by a satellite a section of the cable replaced, why look for a mooring sign? This sub could find anything if given the satellite coordinates. The same spy satellite that saw the Russians replace a section of their cable must have seen them when they first laid the entire cable. We have known all along the cable was there. Perhaps this is why they change their stories, about seeing a sign on the shore. To avoid explaining why they waited to tap the cable till one section was replaced?"

"But they were right." said Rich. "The rest of the cable is shielded, and this one section was replaced, and it is not shielded. You should play chess, not detective. Are you going to move?"

I pushed a pawn and said, "But, Rich, doesn't it all seem a little too coincidental to you? We are to believe that the Russians who knew they needed a shielded cable, made one, but forgot to use it? And it just happens to be a section of the cable that is at a depth that our sub can operate at and we divers can make with the capabilities we have?"

"What are you saying?" asked Rich.

"Was looking for a 'No mooring" sign only a cover story? Did we turn someone? Is someone in Russia working for us and facilitating all this so we can finally get real information 24/7?"

"Maybe they simply ran out of shielded cables." Rich smiled. "I got your rook!"

*(Undersea cables at that time had copper wires in the center, then hard white plastic covering the wires, and then rubber insulation around that. I have heard that shielding a cable can be done by covering the hard white plastic with wire mesh [or a pipe] that is then grounded back at the point of transmission so that the electromagnetic field that the cable gives off will go to ground instead of to the outside of the cable.)

Chapter XX
Professionalism at Sea

CONN

While aboard the *Halibut* in transit to our dive station, we divers had little to do and were allowed to work with submariners on whatever their responsibilities might be. I chose to help the man who worked on the charts and maps. Our position was corrected hourly by reports from transit satellites (similar to GPS) that were obtained from a wire antenna our sub floated to the surface. The reason I chose this job was partly because I thought it would be fun to see our sub's progress through the ocean and into the area of the dives, and partly because I liked being around the CONN.

The center of activity while in transit to and from the dive station was the CONN (the sub's main control room). This was also the only area that would "Rig for Red" every night. In the *Halibut*, as in most submarines, the CONN was on the upper level, in the midsection of the sub and right under the superstructure.

Communications and orders to the entire submarine, including any orders for the weapons control system, were given from the CONN. This included torpedoes and countermeasures, such as motorized decoys and canister bubbles, used to confuse enemy torpedoes. I was told the forward torpedo room had one of the tubes loaded with a nonexplosive torpedo that was a countermeasure. When launched it would maneuver and sound like our sub, even picking up any pings from an enemy vessel, amplifying them, and sending them back so that an adversary would believe they were following a sub rather than a torpedo—in hopes they would depth charge the countermeasure instead of our sub. It is "nice" to have these things, but they are considered last-ditch efforts, and had they ever been used, then everyone on the *Halibut* would have been praying these would work.

Torpedo Room

Next to the CONN were two submariners who manned the many valves for ballast and dives. Next to them were three men who were involved in the steering of our sub. The DO (dive officer, sometimes a chief) sat directly behind and a little above the stern planes man, who had a steering wheel that controlled the depth of the sub, and the rudder planes man, also with a steering wheel, which controlled our direction. Then came the man I helped, who worked on the maps and charts showing our position. Then right next to the CONN was the sonar room.

Stern and Rudder Steering Wheels

The CONN itself had a raised platform about a foot higher than the surrounding area, with two periscopes, and at least one officer on duty.

All of this and much more were crammed into a very small space, in or around the

CONN. I have visited four other submarines and have seen their CONNs, but nothing impressed me as much as the CONN on the *Halibut*.

Twin Periscopes "Rigged for Red"

The orders for speed, depth, and course changes were also given from the CONN by the OOD (officer on deck). And these had to be repeated by those who received them, and, once achieved, the appropriate response was given back to the CONN.

Anyone walking into this area of the CONN would have known immediately that things were different. The tone of the orders being given and the professionalism in which they were carried out were striking, with only limited small talk allowed. Everything at the CONN followed a certain procedure, which was carried out smoothly and efficiently.

I was helping the chart man when there was the 04:00 (a.m.) change of officers at the CONN. The officer coming off duty said with a loud voice, "Lieutenant Smith has the CONN!" And this was routinely recorded in the ship's log.

Speaking just above a whisper, I asked the chart man, "You want me to get our hourly position from the satellite?" He started to answer but was interrupted by the intercom.

"CONN, Sonar. We have a surface contact bearing zero niner five."

"Sonar, CONN. Aye."

"You don't want to disturb sonar right now," said the Chart man. "Wait until they classify their new contact."

"Dive officer, CONN. Come right. Make your course zero five zero."

A watch station man arrived.

"CONN, Watch. May I step up on the CONN?"

"Watch, CONN. Permission granted."

"Sonar, CONN. Have you classified the contact?"

"CONN, Sonar. That's a negative."

"Dive officer, CONN. Make your depth 60 feet" [periscope depth].

Sonar

Water is a better conductor of sound than air, and, in fact, the speed of sound travels four times faster in water than in air. Only a thermocline layer, where the water temperature below it is different from the water temperature above it, will block the sound of ships and subs.

CIA Release

"The U.S. subs also compiled 'signatures' of Soviet submarines, the noise they emit as they move underwater." (Declassified and

Because of the need to maintain silence so a sub cannot be detected, submarines use passive sonar. Active sonar, with its loud pings, will let you know where an enemy vessel is, but also lets the enemy know where you are. Instead, subs only use passive sonar, listening for any sounds in the water. These sounds are then feed into a computer that has been uploaded with the recordings of "acoustic" or "voice signature" of ships, a sort of fingerprint for ships and submarines. These include many from the Russian navy. I was told it is possible to tell not only whose vessel it is but if it was a merchant ship or naval vessel, when it was constructed, and if we could confirm the "voice signature," even the name of ship.

CIA Release

"U.S. intelligence-gathering project that used submarines that penetrated Soviet harbor security and photographed the bottom of Soviet submarines." (Declassified in Part—Sanitized

Though thankfully not common, underwater collisions with foreign submarines have been reported. In this dangerous game of cat and mouse that submarines play, sometimes a sub will follow an enemy sub or even come right underneath it.

The area directly behind the sub is blind to sonar, because of the noise made by the sub's propeller. This sound is called *cavitation*, caused by the little bubbles that make a popping sound as they roll off the edge of the propeller blades. Thus, passive sonar, which only listens for sounds, cannot hear what is directly behind a sub, as the propeller's own noise will mask any other sound that is behind it.

To help a submarine detect what is directly behind it, side-look sonar is used to see what is hidden behind the propeller noise. The sub will change course slightly (some subs make a complete circle) and then "look" (listen) behind it for any possible followers.

Halibut was equipped with side-look sonar, but if a trailing sub stops its propellers, it will not make any sound and thus evade detection.

(The *Halibut* did not tow a sonar listening device. It is possible to attach passive sonar to a cable that is let out from the back end of a submarine. These cables can trail for hundreds of yards behind a sub and listen for any approaching foreign submarine.)

Strange as it may seem to anyone who is not familiar with this, even the style of a submarine's individual propeller blades is most often classified—whether they can change the degree of angle, or even the shape of the blades. When in dry dock, the propellers are even covered by tarps so a satellite can not see them.

Killer Whales

I was up by the CONN helping with the navigation map. The chart man asked me to go to the sonar room to get the hourly satellite report. We use this to compare, and, if need be, correct the penciled-in progress on our map.

The sonar room was only four short steps from where I was helping: everything in that area of the CONN was close together. The sonar room itself was petitioned off from the rest of the CONN by a thin sheet-metal wall. There were two sonar men in the room when I entered, and one was recalibrating a passive-sonar screen. The main sonar technician had headphones on and was turning a dial, listening intently.

"Satellite report?" I said to the assistant.

The assistant reached over and handed me a paper with the coordinates of our sub's position and then said, "We have killer whales on sonar right now. They have been trying to follow us for the last few minutes, but they can't keep up. I guess they can hear us and are curious as to who we are. At any rate, we are hundreds of feet under them."

"Do you run into them very often?" I asked.

"Not much in the middle of the ocean, but they have been heard on location where the dives will be." The sonar technician grinned.

"Seriously?" I asked.

He nodded his head yes.

Should I praise the Lord for "killer" whales?

Killer whales are usually thought of as harmless and playful, entertaining the public at marine parks. Today we are encouraged to call them "orcas." But they have attacked humans, sometimes fatally, including their trainers. They make certain sounds, such as clicking, splashing, whistles, and more, all picked up by our sonar, but they can be silent and dive deeper than our saturation dives. Mature male killer whales average 23 feet in length, and mammals that size could hurt you without even meaning to. Our diving umbilical cables partially float above the seafloor and might look tempting to a killer whale to play with, bite on, or jerk—with a diver still attached.

Chapter XXI
Outskirts of Moscow

Mr. Orlov, the KGB security expert, is at a store buying flowers for his wife, and a man comes up beside him. They do not acknowledge each other's presence, but the other man, who is an American agent, begins speaking to Mr. Orlov without looking at him. "We were hoping you would have had that new cable replaced at the northern port."

Mr. Orlov glances around but says nothing.

"Are you having second thoughts?"

"I have a new situation," says Mr. Orlov.

"Yes, we have heard about your new position; it may be useful in the future."

"I am not talking about that," Mr. Orlov says. "There is a KGB lieutenant who works with spies, both ours and foreign, and he is asking questions about the cable."

The American agent looks concerned but insists, "We put the money in the account you requested, but you have not followed through on your part. We need that unshielded cable at this new location. We have more subs waiting."

Mr. Orlov responds, "Right now is not the best time with this KGB lieutenant breathing down my neck."

With this, the agent takes a different tone and even bumps Mr. Orlov with his shoulder. "Nothing is going to be compromised, is it?"

Mr. Orlov glances around and says, "Put double the amount in my foreign account and I'll send out another unshielded cable for the new location. But no more meetings between us till the deposit is made."

The American agent turns and looks directly at Mr. Orlov and says, "We had a deal!"

"And I have a new situation."

Mr. Orlov then walks away, leaving the American agent standing there. He stops at the checkout counter and pays for his large bouquet.

The sales lady says, "I'm sure your wife will like these."

Then he walks out of the store.

Chapter XXII

God is Working

I was in the secondary control room listening to a song on the eight-track stereo, when Chief came up the ladder from the aft torpedo room.

Chief asked, "How did it go with your dad? You said you were going to try and witness to him before we left port."

"Not so well. The last time I was home, I was on the roof of my parents' house, helping my dad nail down some shingles. I mustered up all my courage and said, 'Dad, have you thought any more about being saved?'

"You know what he did? He stood up and took the hammer that was in his hand and bounced it off the roof. The hammer spun through the air all the way to the ground.

"And then he said, 'Yes I have thought about it!'

"And, as usual, he started cussing. I couldn't get a word in edgeways."

"Sorry to hear that," Chief said.

"Then just before our sub left port, I called my dad on the phone. Something he said over the phone gave me a crack in the door, and I knew I had better go through it because I didn't get opportunities like that from him.

"'Dad,' I said, 'you know God loves you ...' He immediately became upset and said, 'Son, why do you always bother me about this?'

"God gave me the right thing to say to him. 'When you love someone enough, you will tell them what they need to hear.' Then he hung up on me."

Chief said, "I will be in prayer for him."

"Thanks. Hey, Chief, what do you think my chances are of being chosen to be one of the eight divers?"

"There are definitely more than eight of you who want to make these dives."

"How do you know?" I asked.

"I talked to the diving officer about it. He mentioned that you had also asked. I doubt they would pick anyone over 30, so I am not in the running. And it is fine; I have done this before. But just keep praying about it."

The Preacher

The submariner whom I called "Preacher," taught a Bible study, and on Sunday he preached to us. I had never heard preaching before. It wasn't some sermonizing from a denominational textbook, but standing up and declaring God's Word, and it stirred my heart. Teaching is giving out information but preaching has urgency in it. Teaching tells you how to do something but preaching makes you want to do it. Though teaching the Bible is also of our Lord, God chose preaching as one of His main ways to grab hold of people (I Corinthians 1:21).

God was working on this sub. He had called two of us from the *Halibut* to be missionaries and start churches in other countries. Once, maybe twice, our Sunday services had forty men! Incredible when you consider that, at any given time, a third of the men had to be on duty station. We met in the chow hall between meals, as no other place could hold us. When we sang, if the hatches were open, it went through the whole sub. I asked an officer who came regularly to the services if this was normal, and he said that even on an aircraft carrier with thousands of sailors, he had never seen more than eight Christians meeting together.

We were having our Sunday service, and after we sang, Chief asked one of the submariners if he would read a passage from Psalm 107:23–32.

"They that go down to the sea in ships,
that do business in great waters;
These see the works of the LORD,
and his wonders in the deep.
For he commandeth,
and raiseth the stormy wind,
which lifteth up the waves thereof.
They mount up to the heaven,
they go down again to the depths:

their soul is melted because of trouble.
They reel to and fro,
and stagger like a drunken man,
and are at their wits' end.
Then they cry unto the LORD in their trouble,
and he bringeth them out of their distresses.
He maketh the storm a calm,
so that the waves thereof are still.
Then are they glad because they be quiet;
so he bringeth them unto their desired haven.
Oh that men would praise the LORD
for his goodness,
and for his wonderful works
to the children of men!
Let them exalt him also in the congregation
of the people, and praise him in the
assembly of the elders."

When the submariner finished reading the passage he asked, "Would anyone like to thank or praise the Lord for something?"

I said nothing then, but I now praise the Lord because He has used me and let me do these things.

Two of the sailors in the service made comments. One said he had recently trusted Christ. Another shared that though he did not know how a certain problem in his life would turn out, he knew the Lord was going to solve it. Then Chief asked the "Preacher" to speak. The Preacher was in his late 20s, dedicated to the Lord, and I liked listening to his messages.

Preacher

"Glad you are all here. God is doing something on this sub.

"Someday we will all stand in front of a holy God. He won't ask us what church we go to, but He will know if we have trusted His Son Jesus Christ to save us or not.

"Whatever else you are trusting in for heaven, you have to let go of and trust only Christ. There are many good things, such as church and charitable deeds, but *things* cannot forgive sins, only Jesus Christ can.

"I want to read from God's Word. 'For by grace are ye saved through faith; and that not of yourselves: it is the gift of God: Not of works, lest any man should boast' (Ephesians

2:8–9). Salvation is 'the gift of God,' not the gift of a church or the gift of a minister, but it belongs to God. And if you want it, you must go to Him to get it.

"We don't deserve it or work for it, but we must humble ourselves and ask Him for it. Man's way gives the glory to man, by his earning his own salvation, but in God's way, *only* Jesus will receive the glory, because our faith is in Him and what He has done for us, not in ourselves and what we have done. That's why the verse said, 'Not of works, lest any man should boast.' God does not want to listen to us boast to Him about how great we are; He already knows we are sinners.

"Let me ask you all a question. Do you believe a parachute really works? Raise your hand if you do. I can see most all of you believe that. I have another question. How many of you have ever gone skydiving? Only one of you. Well, that means even though you all believe a parachute works, only one of you has ever trusted a parachute.

"For a moment, let the parachute represent Jesus Christ, and the plane represent our religion and good works. In your daily walk, please be good, but good works will never pay for your sins or buy your way to heaven. To trust the parachute, you have to let go of the plane, and to trust Jesus Christ, you have to let go of your baptism, church, and good works. All good things and you should do them all, *but only God's Son can save your soul!*"

"When people say, 'Hey, I believe in God, and if I'm good, I will go to Heaven,' they're not trusting Jesus Christ to save them, but being 'good.' *Let go of the plane!*"

Chapter XXIII
Submarines Rendezvous

One reason for the high interest in our operation was the audacious nature in which it was done—with not one person risking his neck, but the crews of two nuclear submarine meeting in Soviet territorial waters.

There was a prearranged rendezvous point in the Sea of Okhotsk, just inside the Kuril Islands. This rendezvous had each sub at a different depth, to avoid a possible collision. The nuclear submarine USS *Stingray* had already positioned herself in this sea and was waiting and listening for us to come in through the channel. This was to verify that we had made the transit into this Russian sea and were not being followed by an enemy sub.

The *Stingray* was to listen for us and then listen to see if a Soviet sub was behind us. Though it was not expected that a Russian sub would try and sink us in international waters, it was expected that they would try once we entered their territorial waters. If a Soviet vessel, including a destroyer, were to have intercepted the *Halibut*, our other fast-attack submarine was to be the decoy by creating a distraction. She was a newer sub, very fast, and able to outrun Soviet destroyers.

Verification was by listening for the voice signatures of each other's sub. These voice signatures had already been uploaded to both subs' sonar computers before leaving port.

Entering Soviet Territorial Waters

High above the ocean was a US Navy Transit Satellite circling the earth and transmitting coordinates to navy ships and submarines. The *Halibut* was positioning herself in a channel between two islands at the entrance into this sea. It was sunset, and 400 feet below the waves, the *Halibut* was receiving these coordinates via a floating antenna. The antenna was protruding above the waves and slowly moving through the waters toward the channel and then disappeared below the water line.

USS *Halibut*

The main sonar man on our sub was in his late 20s and had graduated top off his class. Over *Halibut*'s intercom, he said, "CONN, Sonar: Our floating antenna has been lowered, and the chart man is verifying the satellite coordinates."

"Sonar, CONN: Aye."

Captain Larson said, "XO, see if we are lined up for the channel."

"Yes, Captain."

Aft Torpedo Room

In the aft torpedo room two divers, Johnson and Nolan, competed to see how many handstand push-ups they could do in one minute, while the other divers were encouraging their favorite. We were in anticipation to hear who would be chosen for the dives, and the competition between us divers sometimes carried over into other areas.

"Johnson, if you can't do any better than that, then you can forget about the dives," Hutchinson said.

Johnson did not respond to his harassing, saving his breath as he continued his competition, but Smith, his friend, did respond. "Hutchinson, when they're done, let's see how many you can do!"

Johnson and Nolan were still competing, but the focus in the aft torpedo room shifted to the dives. In only a few seconds we were put on edge. Their quick replies revealed they had been thinking about the dives.

"Smith, you think you're a shoo-in because you've made these dives before. Well, don't bet on it!" Hutchinson said.

"Real experience outweighs your practice dives any day of the week," Smith responded.

Though all of us were experienced divers, only Smith and Nolan had made the dives in Siberia before, the rest of us had only made practice saturation dives. As they were exchanging comments, Johnson and Nolan finished their competition, but no one noticed.

Johnson, gasping for air, said to Hutchinson, "I won!"

"I'm happy for you," Hutchinson said sarcastically.

All of a sudden it became quiet and I said to Smith and Hutchinson, "Thanks for the entertainment."

Sub intercom: "This is the captain. Rig for ultra-quiet. No talking above a whisper. All are to remain in their bunks."

"You heard the captain. To our bunks." Said a diver.

The CONN, USS *Halibut*

The sub's intercom had been turned off, small talk was no longer allowed, and the pitch of the orders had fallen to a whisper.

The XO was studying the charts, then looked at the Captain and nodded, affirming that we were lined up for the channel.

Captain Larson said, "Dive Officer, make our depth 300 feet."

"Aye, Captain, making our depth 300 feet."

Throughout USS *Halibut*

For the next three and a half hours much of our sub became like a ghost town that had buildings but no people. No one was milling around and the passageways and the chow hall were empty. Only the CONN and Sonar had men at their duty station but they were quiet and had rigged for red. Each watertight compartment on our sub required one man to be at watch station but the rest of us went to our bunks and remained silent. Some would try to sleep or read a book, but many would stare and think about what we were trying to accomplish—to enter Soviet territorial waters without being detected, as our sub glided over their acoustic range.

USS *Stingray*, Submerged and Rigged for Red

Stingray's captain: "XO, stand by the sonar room and let me know when they pick up the *Halibut*."

"Aye, Captain." The XO went to the sonar room, which had two sailors, one on headphones and one looking at the readouts from their computer.

"Sonar, have you picked up anything on the *Halibut*?"

Stingray's sonar man said, "Nothing, XO, only background noise."

The XO walked back to the captain. "Captain, they hear nothing yet. Do you think *Halibut* will wait for a freighter to mask her sound?"

He shakes his head no. *"Halibut* could just let the current take her through the channel."

"So she will not need her screws?" asked the XO.

"Yes, she will need them, but only enough to steer so as to maintain course, but not for speed."

"Captain, the torpedoman's mate is here to see you." said the XO.

The captain of the *Stingray* walked the torpedoman's mate over to one side and said, "You know why we are here, and we hope you and your crew will never be needed, but, it's our job to protect the *Halibut*. So we are going to be ready. The outer doors to torpedo tubes one and four are to be opened now!"

"I have already instructed Sonar that if they pick up any Soviet sub trailing the *Halibut*, they are to listen for the outer doors of their torpedo tubes being opened. If that happens, then we will be a step ahead of them. You understand? Be ready!"

The torpedoman's mate nodded his head, and the captain walked back to the CONN.

Soviet Destroyer

Captain Nikolay was pacing the deck, hoping for some action. His destroyer was slowly moving in an elongated circle at the main point of entry into the Sea of Okhotsk.

"Radio Room, have you any reports from our acoustic range?"

"Nothing, Captain."

"Sonar, what about you? Anything?"

"No, Captain."

USS *Halibut* between the Kuril Islands

No one was making a sound in the area of the CONN. The orders from the CONN were walked to Sonar instead of the usual speakerphone. The XO asked sonar if they could hear the *Stingray*.

Sonar simply responded, "Nothing yet."

The XO then looked toward the captain and shook his head no.

The captain asked the officer on deck (OOD), "Lieutenant, is there a thermocline layer here?"

"Not here, Sir. Maybe once we get into deeper water, we'll find one."

Russian Acoustic Range

On the Kamchatka Peninsula, two technicians were listening for intruders into their territorial waters. In a room on the other side of a glass wall the acoustic officer was seated with his feet up on his desk and playing darts.

One of the technicians brought a paper readout to the acoustic officer and said, "Lieutenant, I have something here that you should look at."

"It doesn't say what it is?" responded the Acoustic Officer.

"Well, it is submerged, and if it is a sub, it is not one of ours."

Acoustic Officer went into the glass rooms to listen for himself. And then he said, "That new destroyer captain, the one at the entrance into our sea, he was insistent that if we picked up anything, we were to give it to him. So send it to him."

Soviet Destroyer

"Captain, Radio Room. We have just received a transmission from our acoustic range, and they have something. But not where we had expected. Instead it is coming in through the next southern channel."

"Is it submerged?" shouted the captain.

"Yes Sir, but they are not sure what it is. They only sent the transmission because you were adamant that on anything new, they were to inform us."

Captain Nikolay walked over to his charts and said, "Show me this channel."

"Captain, it is on the far side of the next island. Even at full speed, it will take us 20 minutes to get there."

Captain Nikolay then belted out orders to his XO. "Chart us a course to this channel and park us right in the middle of it! Officer on Deck, tell the engine room to make full speed."

"Yes, Captain."

USS *Stingray*

"CONN, Sonar: We have a *surface* contact bearing zero niner five."

Stingray's captain and XO looked at each other with surprised expressions. The captain and XO then both went to the sonar room.

"Did you say *surface* contact?" asked the XO.

"Yes, sir! The computer is working on it. But whatever it is, it is definitely Russian."

Stingray's captain asked, "Nothing on the *Halibut*?"

"Sir, we have no submerged contacts at all."

The computer readout was taken by the XO, who glanced at it and handed it to the captain. *Stingray*'s Captain said, "It's a Russian destroyer, Skoryy class, bearing down on us and at full speed. It will be here in fifteen minutes."

XO said, "Sir, we could outrun their destroyer."

"The *Halibut* couldn't," responded the captain. "That destroyer is not coming for us— they couldn't have heard us. We are barely moving. It has to be coming for the *Halibut*. It's the time she should be here. The Russians must have picked her up on their acoustic range."

The sonar man interjected, "Captain, you should know that if the *Halibut* is transiting the channel now, she would not hear that Soviet destroyer till she was past the northern island."

"Let's make some noise!" ordered the captain. "Officer on Deck, make our depth 200 feet. Tell Reactor to bring her to full power and Engine Room to stand by for flank speed."

The OOD looked concerned, hesitated, but began to pass along the orders.

Stingray's XO said, "Captain, the Russians will hear us!"

The captain responded, "Yes, they will!"

USS *Halibut*

"We have a submerged contact, possibly the USS *Stingray*. It's from the area she should be in." The XO relayed the message to the captain and then returned to the sonar room.

"XO, I am sure it is one of our boats. The noise from her screw is definitely US. Just a moment, while the computer spits it out." Out came the readout and the sonar man smiling, said, "Yes. It's the *Stingray*."

"Odd though. She is making more noise than I would have expected for the rendezvous. Sir, I'm afraid the Russian acoustic range can hear her."

The XO informed the captain. The captain asked, "How much longer before we are out of the channel?"

"We are almost out now." The USS *Halibut* continued on her course and headed out into deeper water, dived below a thermocline, and entered safely into the Sea of Okhotsk.

The Rendezvous was Missed!

USS *Stingray* was making noise trying to contact the *Halibut*, but did not realize the *Halibut* had already heard her. The *Halibut* assumed that if she heard the *Stingray*, then the *Stingray* must have heard the *Halibut*. But the *Stingray* never heard the *Halibut*, and the rendezvous was missed. One advantage of the *Stingray*'s loud noise was that it masked the sound of the *Halibut* from both the Russian acoustic range and any enemy vessel in the area.

The USS *Stingray* ended up leaving the Sea of Okhotsk and exited out the nearest channel. She travels far enough out into the Pacific Ocean so that when she radioed US Naval Command, her position would not betray that she has been in the Sea of Okhotsk.

Soviet Destroyer

The Soviet destroyer showed up ten minutes too late. But they were informed by their acoustic range that an American submarine traveling at high speed had exited out through the Kuril Islands and into the Pacific. Captain Nikolay did not waste the opportunity and radioed the Soviet naval base at Vladivostok.

"Tell Admiral Gorshkov that I have just chased an American submarine out of our waters! I doubt they will try that again!"

US Naval Command

When the navy was informed that the rendezvous had not been made, the *Halibut* was then listed as "Missing at sea."

This would have caused a panic in both the *Stingray* and Naval Command. However, the navy hoped the *Stingray* had only not heard the *Halibut*. Naval Command radioed both subs with a new rendezvous time and scheduled a new location (but still inside the Sea of Okhotsk). This meant we had to turn around and go back for a few days and try again to rendezvous with the *Stingray*. And this time we made lots of noise and succeed in the contact.

(I have read that the USS *Halibut* was a noisy sub, and some even say this was the reason she was decommissioned. No, it wasn't! Even before *Halibut*'s last deployment, all on board knew that this was her last run. Because she had come to the end of her nuclear fuel. It would take a year and a half to refuel her, and her sister ship was waiting to take her place. *Halibut* had been tested by our own acoustic range, and at slow speeds she was very quiet. Captain Larson had even said that the *Halibut* was quiet, by the fact that our other submarine in the Sea of Okhotsk was not able to hear us at the first rendezvous attempt.)

Chapter XXIV
Struggling with a Decision

While on our submarine, I wrestled with whether or not I would serve God and about being chosen for the dives. I wondered if somehow the two were connected—serving God and Him allowing me to make the dive. I had trusted Jesus Christ with my soul, but I still wanted to make the decisions on what I was going to do with my life.

Desire

I have read online sites that called us divers "intrepid" for stepping out of a submarine in 400 feet of water—but then turned around and called us "babies" if we did not get chosen to make the dives, saying we had a bad attitude about it. But we wanted to make the dives, and if it is okay to say, *it was fun!* We were well trained, in good shape physically, and chomping at the bit to make one of these dives.

There were 21 saturation divers in our group, known as Deep Dive Team One (DDT1). Not only did most of us want to be selected to be one of the eight divers, we, or at least I, also wanted to be chosen to make the first saturation dive. The first saturation dive was "hook up," or doing what we had gone there for, and the second was "disconnect."

I was up in the DSRV in the secondary control room asking Chief questions about the Bible, and he said to me, "Garry, you ought to go to Bible college."

"Yeah, right, Chief," I replied, laughing. "I have no intention of going to any college, let alone Bible college. I won't fit in there."

Chief said, "God is not looking for perfect people—*there aren't any!* Just those who will let the Lord make them into who He wants."

"OK, Chief. Listen, there is something else I want to talk to you about. We have practiced for more than a year for this one special operation, and I definitely want to be chosen for one of the two saturation dives that are planned. But every time I pray about it, I feel like God is saying to me, 'What if I don't let you make these dives?' I am not hearing any voices, only this impression that He might not let me do this."

Chief asked, "You don't believe God wants you to make these dives?"

"No, not that, or at least I hope He is willing to let me make one of the dives. Chief, I am holding nothing back on this, and I cannot bear the thought of being passed over and someone else taking my place. OK, maybe I'm childish, but for me, being chosen for this is the most important thing in my life.

"And when I pray, I tell the Lord I will live a better life for Him and serve Him if He lets me make one of these dives. But when I ask God, I keep getting the impression, 'What if I don't let you make the dives?'"

Chief asked, "Why is the dive so important to you? You want that medal, the Legion of Merit?"

"Yes, I would like one of those. I accept that, for some people, a medal is not necessary. But what we are doing is important, and that's why they give medals. And yes, I want to do something that others consider 'important.'

"But that's not it. I can live without the medal. It's something else. I don't want someone looking down their nose at me as if I am not good enough, physically or mentally, to make these dives. I want to prove to others, and myself, that I am just as qualified as everyone else. I can do this. It's just jumping in the water to me. And I know the other divers can do it also. Still, some of us won't be chosen. And it makes me heartsick thinking about being rejected.

"The closest thing I can compare it to is when I was in high school and playing second-string football. I was a skinny kid then and tired of being run over by the bigger players. But the few times I played in a game were fun, a real adrenalin rush for me. But most of the season I sat on the bench. I didn't like the feeling it gave me, that I was somehow inferior to others. This is how I feel now about the dives: I want to play, *not sit on the bench!*

"But when I pray about it, I get the impression the Lord only wants to know one thing, 'What if I don't let you make the dive? Will you serve me anyway?' Chief, I know that if I tell the Lord that I will serve Him, even if I don't get what I want, that He will hold me to it."

"Hmm," responded Chief. "By the way, I asked the diving officer again, and he told me it is now down to ten of you that they are going to pick from, and you are still in the running."

I Will Serve You

The next day I was in my bunk praying, when I heard Chief's voice. I climbed out of my bunk to talk to him.

Chief asked, "How you doing? I have been praying for you about the dive.

"Thanks," I said.

"Have you been able to give this into the Lord's hand?"

I nodded my head yes and said, "I prayed and told the Lord I would serve Him even if He does not let me make the dive. But I added on to the end of my prayer, 'God, I really want to do this.'"

Chief half laughed and walked away.

The next day our diving officer walked up to me and only said one thing, "You're making the first SAT dive." He then walked off, leaving me standing there and wondering how such a monumental thing to me could have been resolved in only one sentence.

Chapter XXV
"Keeping Your Cool"

There was something about our sub that I had not expected, limited fellowship. You could talk to anyone but people tended to stay in their own group.

Much of our sub was off limits. From the forward torpedo room till the bulkhead that housed the nuclear reactor, there were the normal off limit compartments. But because our operation was secret to even the crew of the *Halibut*, the computer room, display room and NSA room, were also off limits.

Then from the reactor room aft, was off limits to all but the nukes and divers. This included the engine room and aft torpedo room, one-third of our sub. And the nukes were not allowed in the aft torpedo room. This compartmentalizing of the *Halibut*, though necessary, limited interaction to one's own group, torpedomen, nukes, divers etc., and also limited our space in what was already a very small world.

Try to imagine living in a steel pipe for three months, with no exit, no recreation, no fresh air, and no communication with your girlfriend or family. Sitting on the bottom of a sea hoping that no leaks start with thousands of pounds of pressure per square inch all over the sub. Add to that the anxiety of being in Soviet territorial waters, knowing that if the Russians ever find out that you're there, it will be a very serious problem.

Under conditions like that, it was certainly possible to "fly off the handle". People do and say things they shouldn't, or a practical joke gets out of control. The problem was, there was no way to let off steam until we got back in port.

On the *Halibut*, there were times when a sailor purposely made someone else upset and then went to the chow hall and bragged about it. Such things happen anywhere, but it's worse in a confined environment.

On our sub there was a small room next to the stairway by the entrance into the bat cave. The door to this room was metal, with bars on it, similar to a jail cell. This small room had a few items stored in it but was mostly empty. I notice it every time I walked by, and I finally asked someone, "What is the purpose of that room with the bars on it?"

I was told it really was our sub's jail, and if it was ever needed (which thankfully, it was not), whoever would be put in it would only be served bread and water until the captain released him.

There was one US Marine on board the *Halibut*, who was to some extent a security guard. He had a likable personality, but he served no visible purpose. He was not sub qualified, and he had no duty station that I could discern. The only thing he did was to occasionally run on the treadmill. This marine and the cell were visible reminders that no matter how fed up one might get, discipline would still be maintained.

It was acknowledged by all that we were fortunate to have our cook, as he made the best meals, and even homemade bread. But his job was demanding, and he constantly worked. One time when we were at periscope depth, the *Halibut* was rocked by a surface wave, sending the food from the galley stoves onto the floor. Words and tempers flew.

I was in the aft torpedo room when the tallest diver on our team, someone not used to taking back talk, came in upset. He said it was because the cook had hollered at him. This diver started to say, "Sometimes that cook can … can … well …" But then he stopped his words midsentence and sat down.

No one said anything, thinking it would pass. After about ten minutes, the cook came into the room through the steel hatch wiping his hands on a towel. The aft torpedo room was off limits to him. Still, no one said anything, but we only watched him. He told the diver he was sorry (for which I admired him), and then he stood there in front of the diver, expecting some sort of response. But the diver just looked at him, and then barely nodded his head. Then the cook turned and looked at the rest of us, and then walked out. All this was done without anyone else saying a word. Everyone knew it was not good to let our tempers get out of control in such a small environment.

There was one more thing "added to the mix." Shortly after we entered thc Sea of Okhotsk, the eight of us would be diving were informed by our diving officer. This meant there were some very happy people and some very unhappy people. Oddly, the competition between the divers seemed to grow after the eight of us were picked.

Before the dives, the eight of us who had been chosen shaved off our beards, as they affected the seals on our dive masks. Then a corpsman had us practice giving injections and drawing blood from each other so that if the need arose for this, a medical officer would not have to be "pressed down" into our diving habitat.

Meanwhile, one of the divers showed up who had not been chosen and said he wanted to practice with us. He thought he could be a substitute in the event one of the divers became sick. But the diving officer had not given authority for this, and the corpsman would not permit it. They went back and forth on this about three times. The diver kept giving reasons why it would be a good idea and the corpsman why it wouldn't. Apparently the diver thought if he just forced it, it would work out, but it didn't and the diver was not going to leave.

I thought the corpsman handled it the right way—he just folded his arms and looked down at the ground and said nothing. It was quiet for a few seconds, with the rest of us divers standing there staring at this one diver. Then he left, no one said anything and the corpsman went on as though the other diver had never been there.

I believe I knew how this diver felt, because I would have felt the same way, seeing your dream slip away. I found out later this same diver was assigned to one of the following submarines that took *Halibut's* place. And then it worked out for him as he was chosen to make a SAT dive in Russian waters. He was not a quitter.

To say I was overjoyed at getting to make this dive would be an understatement. Which did not help relations with those around me. One diver who was chosen was still not happy, because he was picked for the second saturation dive. He'd hoped, perhaps expected, to be on the first SAT dive. Even though this diver was put in charge of the team of four divers who would make the second SAT dive, still he was burned about not being on the first SAT dive.

I even started to called him by a new name. "Hey *number two*, how are you doing?" Refereeing to him being on the second SAT dive. This upset him. I shouldn't have done it;

he was really a good guy. But that was the sort of ribbing we gave each other.

He grew tired of it and thought he would get even with me. I was sound asleep in my bunk when I was awakened by "Number Two" and his friend. They both shook me and said, "Garry, wake up! There is bad news! I am sorry to have to tell you, but there has been a change on who is diving."

Normally when I wake up out of a sound sleep, I am confused. But not then, I knew exactly what they were up too. I said, "Oh, Number Two, you mean they are not going to let you dive at all?"

He was immediately upset and left. Now before you judge us for being too juvenile, try living in a submarine for three months. This story I just shared may help prepare you, for there was some tension on our sub. What follows happened only a few days before the dives.

Each day I walked through the length of the sub and fellowshipped with whomever might want to talk. After I made my way back to the aft torpedo room, I saw Jim, a diver friend who had watch. Every compartment on the sub was required to have a watch station to make sure no fires or leaks started. My friend was red faced and visibly upset.

"What's the matter?" I asked.

He named a diver, "Wilson is drawing pictures of my wife!"

We had a large book with blank pages, and whoever wanted to could write a saying or a funny poem or draw pictures in it. This other diver had drawn three or four pictures of Jim's wife. These were not sensual pictures, but of a past argument he'd had with her. Wilson had drawn Jim's wife and wrote what she had said in this book, which was open to anyone to read.

Jim was very upset about it and said, "I want to take a hammer to him!"

I looked at him for a second and realized I needed to do something. I found the book and tore out the drawings of his wife, ripped them up into small pieces, and threw them in a trash can. Then I went to find the master diver, who in our chain of command was over us. I found him in the chief's lounge, but this was off limits to me. So I stood at the door and asked him to come out and talk. But he said, "Later."

This made for an awkward situation because it could not wait. There was another chief in this lounge, if I blurted out what the problem was, the other chief would hear it and it would go through the whole sub. So I asked again, "Chief, it is really important. I need to talk to you, please." What he said next irritated me.

"What's the matter? You afraid we will change our minds and not let you make the SAT dive?"

I knew immediately where this came from. I guess one could say I got payback from Number Two. When I heard the master diver say this, I thought, *OK, I'm just going to blurt it out*.

"Wilson drew some pictures of Jim's wife, and Jim said he wants to take a hammer to him."

The other chief in the room said, "Whoo!" The master diver ran out and asked, "Where is Jim?" I told him and he took off to find Jim. He found him and calmed him down. Later I was going through the chow hall and saw our master diver sitting at a corner table with Wilson. They were the only two at the table and the master diver was dealing with the situation.

Neither one of these divers were bad people; they were just enduring living in a submarine for three months.

Chapter XXVI
The Dives

Unforeseen and surprising
Events at the site of the dives.

Courtesy of H I Sutton, Covert Shores.

Divers in the drawing are placing a POD used to store recordings, but we used "clamps" and the recordings were stored on the *Halibut*. On the seafloor is the cable, and to the right is a ROV [Remotely Operated Vehicle] filming it. Us divers called it the "Eye".

CIA Release

"**Ivy Bells** ... an undersea cable linking one part of the Soviet Union to the other across the Sea of Okhotsk, was bugged by a device set out by a submarine. A submarine pulled near it and frogmen went out and attached a device ..." (Declassified and Approved for Release 2011/12/21,   CIA-RDP90-00965R000100310013-6)

Getting Ready

Though most sailors on the sub did not know where we were or what we were getting ready for, all knew the *Halibut* was "parked" on the seafloor and the dives were about to begin. The crew of the *Halibut* had got us safely into this Russian sea, and they wanted the dives to be a success. Now the spooks, project officers, and divers took center stage. A whole year's planning was about to be tested. It fell on us divers to implement this, and we were savoring the moment. During this time the divers began "startup," with check-off lists to bring both diver control rooms online.

Display Room

All eight divers, plus the master diver and diving officer, were assembled in the display room. Before this meeting, I had only caught glimpses of the display room, when its door was open, for normally it was off limits. The display officer was one of the two project officers on board, the other was the diving officer.

The location of the display room is shown on the following drawing, right above the aquarium.

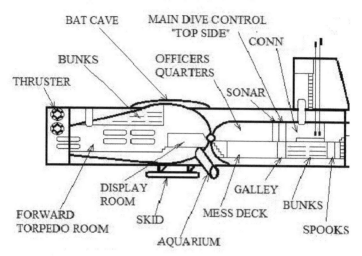

INTERIOR USS *HALIBUT* (SSN-587)

BAT CAVE   MAIN DIVE CONTROL
                "TOP SIDE"
                        CONN

BUNKS   OFFICERS
             QUARTERS
THRUSTER
                        SONAR

DISPLAY   GALLEY
ROOM   BUNKS
FORWARD   MESS DECK
TORPEDO ROOM   SKID   SPOOKS
           AQUARIUM

The computer room on the *Halibut* had a reel-to-reel system, a dinosaur by today's standards. This computer was used in conjunction with the Fish and side thrusters that helped position it. But the display room had always been a curious place to me, looking more like what I thought a computer room should look like. There we were shown the film footage from the Fish, of the cable and its inline amplifier.

The display room had a large screen, perhaps six feet across by four feet high. And their equipment was able to draw on this screen an exact replica of the cable and amplifier with amazing detail. This was more helpful than a picture, for I saw something on this that I had not recognized on the film footage from the Fish. It appeared to be some sort of pipe about two feet long by one inch wide. I asked the officer in charge of display what it was, and he said they did not know but that they were interested in it and wanted us to bring it back.

Tapping Devices

During our training dives off the California coast, we had practiced with the "clamps" (tapping devices that were put on the cable). Similar to how an auto mechanic would place a clamp around a spark plug wire to see if it has an electrical current running through it.

These clamps we used for the taps were easier to put on and take off than the old wrap-around-wire type. Each clamp was about three feet long by five inches in diameter and painted yellow. One side of the clamp could be opened, and we would place the cable inside the clamp and then close the clamp around the cable.

These clamps also had a metal wire that pulled a quick release on the clamps and detached them from the cable. So that should the Soviets ever bring their cable to the surface and inspect it, they would not find our recording clamps. And if the *Halibut* ever felt threatened by a Soviet ship, she could, in an emergency, lift off the seafloor immediately and leave. This would leave the clamps hanging off the bottom of the sub. Though not an ideal situation, it would at least be possible for her to leave without sending divers out to disconnect the clamps.

It was necessary to position the *Halibut* near to the cable because the clamping devices had a relatively short wire that connected them back to the sub. We were to put seven of these clamps on each side of the amplifier. The more clamps the better for a clearer, stronger signal. If the clamps were not placed on both sides, we would only be recording communications from one direction.

Display showed us a couple more drawings from a zoomed-out position of the overall site and approximately where our sub was positioned next to the cable. On the display room's drawings of the cable, and their projected placement of our sub, the sub and cable appeared to be very close together, especially at the bow of the sub. I made no comment about this, for *Halibut* had already been winched down on her anchors (called "mushrooms") and was sitting on her skids. But I was curious to see just how close we were to the cable.

When we were done, the display officer wished us success. Our diving officer thanked him for the briefing and then shouted out four of our names. "Nolan, Matheny, Smith, and Hutchinson. You four divers who will be making the first saturation dive. I will meet with you in the aft torpedo room. Let's go!"

Chow Hall

On the way to the aft torpedo room, all four of us divers, plus the diving officer and master diver passed through the chow hall.

COB said, "Hey, guys, we'll see you in a week. Good luck!"

Nolan said, "Thanks, COB."

The cook hollered, "Bring me back some crabs and I will cook them up for you."

As we left the chow hall, Chief was waiting for me to pass through, I shook his hand and said, "I am still thanking God He let me do this."

Aft Torpedo Room

The medical diving doctor, who had also gone through saturation dive school, entered the aft torpedo room.

The master diver said, "Guys, line up for your final medical check."

The four of us divers lined up, and the medical diving doctor spent more time looking over Hutchinson, the second man in line, and asked, "How long have you had this sore throat?"

Hutchinson responded, "A couple of days. It's nothing. It doesn't bother me at all."

The doctor took another look and said, "Sorry Hutchinson, but I cannot in good conscience recommend you to be on this dive."

Hutchinson insisted, "I am fine. Really."

The diving officer raised his voice and said, "Hutchinson, step out of line!"

The ejected diver was clearly hurt but said nothing and left.

The master diver shouted into the engine room at a submariner. "I want you to double time it down to the mess decks and get Farinella. He is scheduled to make the next SAT dive. Tell him he is being bumped up to make the first SAT dive and to get down here now!"

The medical doctor next checked me, and when I passed I give a sigh of relief. Then the next diver in line was checked, and when done, the replacement diver arrived, stood in line, and he also passed.

Diving Officer said, "Thanks, Doctor. We will not be needing you now."

The doctor left and the diving officer said, "We need to go over the schedule of the two saturation dives. They will be a week each and 45 days apart. The recordings of real-time conversations will be made between these two dives. Our NSA analysts tell us they expect at least eighteen channels on this one military cable.

"Things are subject to change, but for now the plan is for two water entries during this first saturation dive. Two divers will enter the water together, and the other two divers will tend their umbilical cords. Then on the second water entry, those who tend will enter the water.

"Nolan and Matheny will be the first two divers to enter the water. Nolan will be designated Red Diver, or lead diver, and Matheny will be Yellow Diver. We will be making recordings of these dives, and though you may listen to them afterward, they will remain classified. You will be diving between windows in the tides to prevent fighting the currents and for better visibility.

"We will take extra time to press you down to depth to help your body be better acclimated to the pressure. This will take all night, so try and get some sleep. When you awake, it should be morning topside on the Sea of Okhotsk."

Master diver spoke up, "The captain is coming in. Stand to attention."

The captain entered and said, "At ease."

"Well, this is what we are here for. I want you to know I will be closely following these dives. I wish you success, and I will meet you back here in seven days."

Then up the stern escape hatch we went and through the cramped secondary control room, manned by two saturation divers and into our diving chamber.

Russian Acoustic Range

The technicians were surprised by a visit from Captain Nikolay of the Russian destroyer, who was very upset. Acoustic Lieutenant said, "Captain Nikolay, it is a surprise to see you. Is there a problem?"

"Yes, there's a problem all right! I'm not looking good right now at Naval Command. I understand you have been telling them that the Americans tricked me. You said the sub I chased out of our sea was a decoy to distract my attention from another American sub that slipped in."

"Look for yourself. These readouts are from the night that American sub exited out into the Pacific. That same night we originally heard a very faint sound in the channel that we radioed you about. Later, after the American sub exited out into the Pacific, our technicians went back over the recordings and found this same faint signal again, on the same course but farther out in the Sea of Okhotsk. It is not possible it was the same sub as the one you chased after."

Captain Nikolay asked, "Why didn't you say something to me then?"

"When the American sub exited, she was so loud that she masked everything in the channel. It was not until she passed the outer islands that this faint sound showed up again."

"Have you heard this sub since then?" asked Captain Nikolay.

"No. Our technicians have been looking for it, but most likely this sub is under a thermocline layer. And that sub would be expected to have changed course by now. A sub in a position like that would hear you before you would hear it."

"Give me these readouts. I'll have my sonar man compare them," replied Captain Nikolay, and he leaves as he came, upset!

First Saturation Dive

The third room of the habitat was flooded during transit to the dive station. So that morning, the first item of operation was to pressurize this compartment and remove all the seawater. Once the pressure was equalized between the third and second compartments (where we divers sleep), the metal door was opened. A strong rush of cold saltwater air came in from the freezing 27-degree sea, waking us up like a slap on our faces. A reminder we were not on a training dive. Everyone had a serious look, being fully alerted to what was expected of us.

We entered this third room and started getting dressed into our dive rigs. Then the 140-degree water began pumping between our two wet suits, and once full, the hot water started spilling out around our wrists and neck, falling down to the metal grate we were standing on.

Problem

The dive tenders using the speaker in second room said, "Topside, Tenders: We cannot get the speaker in the dive station [third room] to work. The connecting socket appears to have been clogged up. We will have to communicate with you using the speaker in the second room. This means you will have to speak really loud if we are to hear you, because we will be in the third compartment tending.

"And, Topside, be advised that because of this, when the divers are in the water, they will not be able to speak to us or us speak to them."

Main Diver Control was watching the tenders on their TV screen and said, "Tenders, Topside: We understand. But the divers will still be able to communicate with us using their headphones. Let's try a mic check with the diver's helium speech descrambler."

"Red Diver, Topside. Do you read me?"

"Topside, Red Diver. Loud and clear."

Then I, as Yellow Diver, acknowledge the same.

This procedure of stating the name of whom you were addressing and then your designation of Red or Yellow Diver was standard and seldom deviated from. But when we divers talk to each other, we just spoke normally. Other than these checks, the communications with Topside was infrequent, except to report a problem or Control asking about our progress.

First Water Entry

"Red Diver, Topside: Are you ready to move out?"

"Topside, Red Diver: Entering the water."

After he entered the frigid waters, I followed, and the tenders started letting out our cables. It was about 40 feet from where we enter the water to the seafloor, and I was enjoying it! We were done with our dress rehearsals and had made it past all the hurdles, and I was doing my heart's desire.

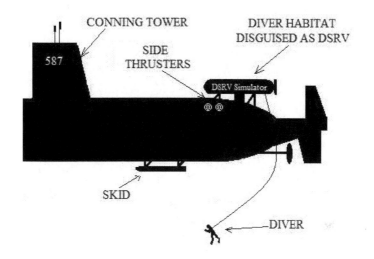

CONNING TOWER

SIDE THRUSTERS

DIVER HABITAT DISGUISED AS DSRV

587

DSRV Simulator

SKID

DIVER

One of the things I liked to do when I dove at the Island of Diego Garcia, and later at Guam, was to drift down backward to the seabed. I would have my back toward the seafloor and my face looking up at the surface of the water and watch the bubbles from my dive rig go through my fins on their way to the surface. We had negative buoyancy with the lead weights in our wet suits, and it would take less than a minute to reach the bottom. But on our mission, there were no bubbles from our dive rigs, no surface to see—only the blackness of the sea.

It was morning topside on the Sea of Okhotsk, but this did little to help light up the seafloor 400 feet below. We had started our first dive right after the current had subsided, and there was still silt in the seawater. Our visibility in the icy-cold water, even when using our lights, was at best only six feet. Though, when the silt settled down, we could see a few feet more. When next to our sub, we could see even more, with the aid of the lights that were on the bottom of the *Halibut*.

The sea itself held little scenery at 400 feet; the silt and sand at the bottom were gray in color. There were some strange-looking fish about 18 inches long, with heads almost half the size of their bodies, eyeballs bigger than a human's, and huge mouths. These fish were not afraid us; they swam right up to us and stared. Some even sat in the silt on the sea bottom, still gazing up at us—eerie! One tried to swallow my flashlight, but I knocked him off. There were also some giant king crabs, about two feet across, slowly walking on the seafloor. Other than those, I saw no other sea life.

The Russian cable could not be seen when we were next to the sub because of the darkness of the sea. But we knew it was close, maybe 30 feet from us, so we swam at a right angle away from our sub until we found the cable. It was three inches in diameter (not five inches, as is commonly reported). Thirty feet up the cable, we found the amplifier, with its strong signal that would make it possible to do the taps.

Ours for the Taking

There lying before us, was the "mother lode" of intel flowing through that one cable. I'd heard that it cost *one billion dollars* to get us to this point. But for a few seconds, we just floated there in the sea, looking at it. The Russians didn't know we were there, nor anyone else. All these secrets were for the taking, 24 hours a day, for as long as we stayed. And we were just staring at the cable, with the blackness of the sea all around us. It was as though we needed someone to tell us,

"OK, guys, do something!" Then Red Diver said, "Well, I guess I should get a clamp."

While he swam back to the sub to open a panel that had the tapping clamps, I inspected the forward skid to see if the cable, which was parallel to the sub, may have veered off toward the bow, as it appeared in the drawings in the display room.

I follow the cable toward the bow, and, yes, it went right under the front port skid! *Halibut* weighs five thousand tons, which was divided up on the four skids. So in theory, over a thousand tons of metal were cutting into the cable. This was one time I deviated from the standard communications procedure—this time I just said, "Topside, we got a problem!"

The master diver was manning the phones in the Main Diver Control, and he also did not follow the normal procedure, which should have been: "Yellow Diver, Topside: What is it?"

Instead, he said, "What, Garry?" He could read the tone of my voice and knew it was a real problem.

"The forward port skid is sitting on the cable." I said.

"No!" was his one-word response.

"Topside, yes, it is!"

For the next few minutes, Main Diver Control and the captain discuss what they should do. Then someone suggested we take one of the clamps and see if we could get a recording. If we had cut through the cable or shorted it out, there would be no signal running through it. We gave that a try, and the spooks from NSA, who were manning the readout on their screens, phone Main Diver Control and told them they had a good recording. Then us divers who were in the darkness and quietness of the sea, heard over our intercom loud cheers from the inside of our sub.

We had not cut through the cable—but it was still a problem. The seabed was not that soft and had rocks in it. The *Halibut*, when sitting on her skids, could rock from side to side if a surface storm was large enough, as could happen in the Sea of Okhotsk.

On one of the training saturation dives off the coast of San Francisco, while sitting on the seafloor at 420 feet, a bad surface storm rocked *Halibut*. This rocking was enough to lift the sub off the skids on one side and then rock back and lift her off the skids on the other side.

There was also a concern that if we tried to lift the *Halibut* off the seafloor, she might not lift smoothly off the seabed, but sway as she broke free and possibly cut the cable.

It was also deemed too risky for another reason. Before I was assigned to the *Halibut*, on one of the dives at location, a dangerous situation arose. At that time, the dives were made with the *Halibut* floating a few feet above the seafloor but held in position by her anchors. The sea is never completely motionless, which caused the *Halibut* to sway. During one of the dives the chain to the forward anchor broke! The sub was then at the mercy of the sea, while the divers were still in the water. One of the divers looked up, and to his surprise, he saw the bow of the *Halibut* coming at him! Obviously a dangerous situation. The crew of the *Halibut* was able to regain control of the sub, and the divers were able to reenter the habitat safely. After that, divers were not allowed in the water while the sub was held in place with only her anchor chains. And we would need to be in the water in order to move the cable out from under the skid. Therefore, raising the *Halibut* at the bow was not an option.

Before Topside could make any decision on what to do, they wanted us to explain how the cable entered under the skid and how far it was till it came out the other side. This first water-entry dive was cut short because of this unexpected problem, and we returned to our habitat. When we returned to the dive chamber, Red Diver made sketches of exactly where the cable entered under the skid, and these were sent to the Main Diver Control.

Second Water Entry

On this water entry a problem occurred— a problem no one had ever considered a possibility.

The second water entry was tasked with two jobs. First, clear away the cable from the port skid, and second, to film what we were doing.

Diver Control decided that an underwater fire hose would be used to clear the seabed away from the cable and pull it free. We were well prepared and had such a hose stowed inside a panel on the bottom of the sub. Red Diver was picked to go back in again on the second dive, as he was the only one who had operated this underwater fire hose before. While he and another diver headed out on this second dive, the other remaining diver and I tended their umbilical cables.

Much of the second water entry was taken up with clearing away enough sand, silt, and rocks to move the cable out from under the skid. The cable itself was bent but not cut into.

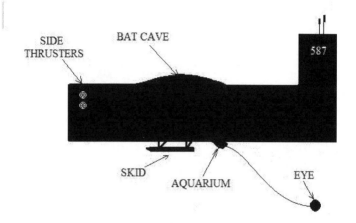

Then they were to film everything, so they brought out the swimming eyeball (Eye) through the aquarium. The Eye would film the cable, amplifier, and the one clamp to show to higher-ups in Washington, D.C. This three-foot round Eye, with its thrusters, could maneuver well enough by itself if there was no current from the tide. It received its electrical current via a cord that was let down through the aquarium, and if need be, a diver could untangle its cord.

Our NSA spooks had special equipment set up that could take all the different channels running through the cable and separate them. So when the NSA analysts back in the States started deciphering, they would not be listening to all the channels at once, which would be like listening to 18 people speak at the same time. But our NSA analysts were able to separate each conversation, even though the recordings had come from the outside of this Soviet cable.

We used the inductive mode of recording, as we were not splicing or cutting into the cable. And if someone could pick up a signal from the outside of a cable, produced by its electromagnetic field, then the reverse was also true. If another source of electricity (the Eye, with its thrusters, lights, and cameras) came close to the cable, it could also project a signal onto the cable. The spooks, who were observing their screens in our sub, notice that the Eye was causing some static on the cable. Not just sound, but also making the readout look fuzzy. But they still could receive all the channels off the cable, each one being displayed on the same screen, parallel to each other.

But then, unexpectedly, a diver's fin appeared on one of the NSA analyst's screens! Then the diver's leg and then both fins and the trunk of his body appeared, and this image of the diver then swam across the analyst's screen!

In a panic the NSA analyst took off running through the sub on his way to the CONN. (He later told me he knocked over a man on his way down the narrow passageway.) He raced up the ladder and into the CONN, hollering, "Shut it off! Shut off the Eye *now!*"

The NSA analyst explained to the captain that there was enough of an electromagnetic field generated by the Eye (when it came close to the cable) to project a fuzzy image onto the cable. A diver had swum between the cable and the Eye, and wherever the diver's body blocked the electromagnetic field of the Eye, it was no longer picked up by the cable. As a result, on the screen, the fuzzy static was only seen around the outline of his body, thus showing the outline of the diver's image.

The concern was, that those who were

using this cable might also have watched this at the Soviet Pacific Fleet base at Petropavlovsk, on the Kamchatka Peninsula, or in Siberia, at Vladivostok.

The display officer came to the CONN and talked to the captain and Main Diver Control about what had happened. "Captain, the equipment and screen of the NSA are a special design. Though the Russians could make something like this, they would have no need for it. The Russians only need telephone receivers to listen to someone on the other end of their cable. But because we are taking this from the outside of the cable, we needed to verify that the different channels are each being separated and not mixed together. So the Russians could not have seen the diver because they would have no need for such equipment like this."

(According to the History Channel documentary *Blind Man's Bluff*, the submarine that took *Halibut*'s place was reported to have slammed down on the cable during a storm. But this did not alert the Soviets, the same documentary acknowledged that it was Ronald Pelton who gave away this operation, not a storm or some unforeseen problem.)

Halibut's Sonar Man

"Captain, on sonar we picked up a Russian destroyer that is using active sonar pinging into the sea. He is several miles away from us and no threat now, but I thought I should bring it to your attention."

"Yes," said the captain, "and keep me informed if he comes any closer to us."

USS *Stingray*

The captain of *Stingray* said, "XO, I want you to take the CONN. But be advised that the Russian destroyer that tried to follow us out of the Kuril Islands is back and pinging on the seafloor. It is doubtful she will find us under this thermocline layer, but the *Halibut* is above the thermocline. Still, that destroyer would have to be almost on top of the *Halibut* to pick her up sitting on the seafloor. "

XO asked, "How far off is it?"

"Too far off right now to be any threat; it is near to the area where *Halibut* first entered this sea. But we will need to keep an eye on her. That destroyer is probably looking for the *Halibut*. Sonar told me the *Halibut* may never have heard that destroyer the night she entered this sea, since we came between where we believed *Halibut* was and that Russian destroyer. Thus, we masked not only the noise of the *Halibut* from the destroyer but we would have also masked the sound of the destroyer from the *Halibut*. *Halibut* would not know they are looking for her."

XO responded, "Maybe that destroyer is only looking for more intrusions into their sea."

"It is possible, but be aware of it. You have the CONN."

Last Water Entry

This third water entry started off good. Only one clamp had been attached, and we had several more to put on. Also we had not yet placed even one clamp on the opposite side of the amplifier. Therefore we were only getting one-way communications and had not achieved one of our main goals of this mission: two-way communications.

Both of us who had tended for the previous dive were picked to make the third, and final, water dive of this first round of saturation dives, and this time, I was designated Red Diver.

On this third dive, we were to finish putting on the rest of the clamps. We entered the water and went straight to where the clamps were stowed. I took one out and went to the cable, found the amplifier, and put the clamp on the other side of the amplifier.

"Topside, Red Diver: I have placed the clamp on the far side of the amplifier. You want to check with the spooks to see if they have a recording from the other side?"

A couple of minutes passed, and once again we heard, over our diver intercoms, a cheer come up from the Main Diver Control.

Then Topside said, "Great, guys! The signal is coming in really strong from off that amplifier. There is going to be some happy people back home." The 1975 deployment of the *Halibut* was the first to achieve these two-way communications.

While Yellow Diver was putting on the clamps, I looked for what I thought was a pipe we had seen on the screen in the display room. I knew approximately where it should be and only swam a short distance until I found it. It turned out not to be a pipe but the hard, white plastic core from the center of the cable. Apparently when the Soviets had spliced in the new section of the cable, they had dropped a piece overboard, and it landed on the seafloor just a few feet from their amplifier.

This center core of the cable had six or seven copper wires, each one about an eighth-inch thick, twisted together on the inside of the hard, white plastic. We divers wanted to cut it into pieces as souvenirs, but the project officers wanted all of it.

Red Light!

We were almost finished and working on the last couple of clamps, when on the inside of my face mask, I saw a red light. This light was triggered by a decrease in pressure from our come-home bottle for emergency return. So either my hose had been bent sharply enough to block the flow of gas, or somehow it had been cut. I knew it was not a problem with the push-pull system that sends the gas to us, because Yellow Diver was not having any problem.

I immediately said, "Topside, Red Diver: I have a red light!"

The quick, calm reply was, "Red Diver, Topside; return to the Dive Station." Those who were over us were professionals. They knew that the tone of their voice could calm someone down and assure them. Nonetheless, I had a red light in my face, which told a diver, *Go back to the dive chamber or you die!*

USS *Stingray*

Stingray's sonar man said, "Captain, you said to tell you if there was an aspect change on the Russian destroyer. Well, she has stopped pinging, but she has also started a much wider loop. If she continues on her present course, the destroyer will be near the *Halibut* in a little more than ten minutes."

"How near?"

"It is hard to say, but perhaps within a half mile of *Halibut*. But like I said, the destroyer stopped her pinging."

The captain ordered, "CONN, Captain: Let's go shallow above the thermocline. And tell forward torpedo room to ready torpedo tube number three."

USS *Halibut*

Halibut's sonar man said, "Captain, that Russian destroyer I told you about before has moved out of its search area. It now seems to be headed fairly close to us. It is not moving in a straight course, so it is hard to judge how close, but definitely closer than before. Perhaps within a mile of us, and she will be here in a few minutes.

"But that destroyer is no longer pinging. Apparently she has stopped her search."

"Keep me abreast of her movement." The captain then ordered over the sub's intercom: "This is the captain; go to all quiet." Then *Halibut*'s captain stepped over to Main Diver

Control and said to the diving officer, "Tell the divers to get out of the water now!"

"Yes, Captain."

"Yellow Diver, Topside: stop whatever you are doing and return to Dive Station now!"

Diving Officer then said to the captain, "Sir, be advised. Red Diver is already coming back; he had a red light come on in his helmet."

"How serious is this?"

"Something has malfunctioned. It could be his diving rig, or his gas supply has been blocked. Red Diver has an emergency return bottle for this. We're timing him and if he goes straight back, he should make it."

Soviet Destroyer

Captain Nikolay was upset because his active sonar was not operating. And then loud pings began to echo from the destroyer.

The destroyer's sonar man said over the ship's intercom, "Captain, Sonar: You can hear we have the active sonar fixed. Do you want us to keep pinging?"

Captain Nikolay retorted, "Yes!"

Halibut's Divers Were in the Water

Pings from the Russian destroyer could be heard by the divers and were growing louder. The pings were also starting to affect the communications between the divers and Topside.

I had all 350 feet of my umbilical cable out, and the communication box in the third room of the dive chamber did not work. I had no way to tell them I was on emergency return and to help bring in my umbilical cable.

"Topside, Yellow Diver: *What's the noise?!*"

"Yellow Diver, Topside: We have a visitor. Get back in as quickly as possible."

Dive Tender

Dive Tender, using the communication box from the second room, asked, "Topside, Tender: What's the pinging from?"

"We will explain later. Just get the divers in, especially Matheny, he has a red light."

Red Diver

I was a few minutes ahead of Yellow Diver and reached the side of the sub. I swam up from the seafloor to the top of the *Halibut*, dragging all 350 feet of my umbilical cable, which was weighing on me. As soon as I reached the top of the sub, I went aft to find the DSRV. The visibility was still poor, about five feet without my light. The tenders had started to bring in my cable, but because there was a slight current in the water, my cable drifted out in the sea and pulled on me from a right angle. This made it hard to hang on to our sub as the surface near to the DSRV was slippery, and the only thing to grab hold of would be a leg of the DSRV.

I glanced at the red light in my face mask, which was reminding me I was running out of time. I made it to the first leg of the DSRV but had been fighting my umbilical cable, which was now causing me to slide off the top of the sub. Trying to prevent myself from slipping off the sub, I went on the inside of the first leg of the DSRV. (This was a mistake, I will explain later.)

I pulled up some of my umbilical cable so it would not drag me back and then tried to reach the next leg of the DSRV. I only went a few feet before my umbilical cable stopped moving, not budging at all.

Then suddenly my umbilical cable yanked me backward! I was at a loss to understand how this could be happening. My feet landed back onto the leg of the DSRV, which prevented me from sliding back any farther. Once again I pulled up on my cable, about 30 feet, giving me enough slack to make a dash for the next leg coming down from the DSRV. I made it!

From there I saw the light shining down in the water from the entry point back into the dive chamber. I pulled up a few more feet of my umbilical cable, intending to push off this last leg. But inexplicably I was again pulled backward and with a sharp pull! This time my face mask slammed into the leg of the DSRV. I hurriedly grabbed back on to this leg to prevent getting dragged back even farther.

I had made a hundred umbilical cord dives and never had this happen before. So who was pulling me away from the dive chamber? And what was it that had caused my gas flow to be blocked and triggered my emergency bottle? I was now remembering what the sonar man had told me about killer whales being in the area, and I wondered if one of them had found my umbilical cable and had decided to "play with it."

The Russian destroyer's pings were increasing in intensity. The red light was still shining in my face, reminding me I had possibly only one minute left. But I was being pulled backward from where I needed to go, and the thought occurred to me, *Am I getting back?*

Dive Tenders

The tenders, who were trying to bring me back in, had my umbilical cable jerked out of their hands! "What is going on?!" asks one of the tenders. "Yellow Diver would not have pulled back Red Diver's cable, and why would Red diver do it?" But mindful of Topside's order to "especially" get Red Diver in, the tenders grabbed hold of my cable and tried again.

Red Diver

Once more I was jerked backward but managed to hang on to the leg of the DSRV. Again I pulled up a few more feet of my cable and pushed off the last leg of the DSRV to try and made it to the entry point. Thankfully, this time I make it, and a minute later, Yellow Diver follows. Once back inside, the tenders hurriedly started taking off our suits and equipment.

Yellow diver said, "You all heard the pings. The Russians know we're here!"

One of the tenders said, "Hey, the pinging has stopped."

The four of us divers listened momentary for the pings. We were not sure what to make of the silence, but being inside of the main dive chamber (where we decompress) would be the safest place.

I said, "I don't know if our sub is leaving, but she won't lift off the bottom until we have closed the outer chamber door." All four of us then quickly enter our dive chamber and shut the metal door.

Soviet Destroyer

Captain Nikolay asked over the ship's intercom, "Who stopped the pinging?!"

The destroyer's sonar man responded, "Captain, good news! Our assistant sonar man has been going over that readout you have from our acoustic range. And right before I started the pinging back up, he had come across a faint sound identical to the readout you gave us! We turned off the pings to see if we could hear it again. And not only have we found it but also that same American fast-attack sub you chased out before. They are both less than two kilometers from here!"

"Great! Give the duty officer the coordinates. And if you can follow those subs using passive sonar then keep using it." Captain Nikolay then gave chase at flank speed.

USS *Stingray*

Stingray's Captain and XO area standing outside the Sonar Room. "Captain, the destroyer is giving chase!" said the sonar man.

Stingray's captain smiled and said, "Officer on Deck, let's get our sub out into the Pacific."

Soviet Destroyer

Over the intercom, the destroyer's radio man said, "Captain, our acoustic range has radioed to tell us they also hear both subs, and I told them we are already pursuing them."

The captain asked, "Sonar, how far away is the faster sub?"

The sonar man hesitated, and then said over the intercom, "Captain, I think you better come here."

Captain Nikolay, irritated, rushed to the sonar room and said, "What?"

"Captain, that fast-attack American submarine is moving through the channel, and we will never catch her. But the slower sub was not a sub at all. It was a countermeasure."

"Countermeasure?!"

"I'm afraid so. It is no longer making any sound, and I heard it hit the seafloor. The sound it made at impact with the seabed was too small to be anything more than a countermeasure."

"We were told at sonar school that the Americans were believed to be working on such a countermeasure. It is designed to give off the same sound as their sub, and it plays this into the water. In other words, we have been tricked. Captain, I'm sorry about this."

Captain Nikolay blurted out, "I'm not sorry! I just proved that there was no second submarine. The Americans are only using countermeasure. And the only ones who have been tricked around here are those from our acoustic range. And again I have chased an American sub out of our sea!"

Chapter XXVII
The Head of the KGB

CIA Release

"Mr. Faulkner said the $35,000 was a 'very, very minimal' payment compared with the value of the secrets that Mr. Pelton had compromised." (Declassified in Part—Sanitized Copy Approved for Release 2012/10/04: CIA-RDP91-00561-R000100120029-7)

CIA Release

"Mr. Pelton told F.B.I. agents last year in two interviews that he took no classified documents into the embassy." (Declassified in Part—Sanitized Copy Approved for Release 2012/02/29: CIA-RDP90-00965R000201830069-6)

Head of the KGB

Mr. Sokolov, the head of the KGB, has summoned Lieutenant Mirgayas Volkov to his office. Lieutenant Volkov rushes in, excited to meet the head of the KGB. "Mr. Sokolov, it is a pleasure to finally meet you!" Mr. Sokolov motions for Lieutenant Volkov to take a seat. Seated beside the desk is Mr. Orlov, the security expert of the KGB.

"This is Mr. Orlov; he oversees our security. I believe you know him."

"Yes, we have talked over the phone." responds Lieutenant Volkov.

But Mr. Orlov does not get out of his chair to greet Volkov or speak to him but only looks in the lieutenant's direction.

"I have gone over your proposals. They are interesting, especially your request to station one of our destroyers at the entrance into the Sea of Okhotsk. I have been informed by Admiral Smirnov of the Soviet Naval Command that your recommendation may be needed after all. Have you heard?"

Volkov shakes his head no.

"Yes, apparently the Americans did try to enter our sea. At any rate, one of our destroyers blocked them and then chased their submarine out into the ocean."

"Great! I am happy to hear this," says Volkov. "Have you seen all that Mr. Pelton gave to us? It's all written there in my brief. This is a real eye-opener to our vulnerabilities. I hope you can see the needs from my proposals. I believe these should be implemented without delay."

Mr. Sokolov taps his desk with Lieutenant Volkov's folder. And Mr. Orlov sits tight-lipped, staring at Volkov.

But Lieutenant Volkov is excited and continues: "Our cable in the Sea of Okhotsk has almost 20 channels of military communications, in just this one cable. All the Americans would have to do is lay a fiber-optic line from our cable to one of their islands. And then they could listen to us live, not just from recordings. In the event of a war, our naval and submarine base in the Sea of Okhotsk would be one of the first alerted. But with the Americans tapping us, we would, in actuality, be alerting them.

Right now we are test launching the SS-20 missile from Siberia to the Kamchatka Peninsula. This is the one we hope to station in Eastern Europe. All this information is presently being carried through our cable in the Sea of Okhotsk. The Americans would know the strengths and weaknesses of our missiles, details of our navy's maneuvers, and learn of our plans in the event of war. But we have even more locations with cables, and they are all vulnerable. They are tapping us with something called the inductive mode ..."

The head of the KGB waves his hand to stop Lieutenant Volkov in midsentence. "You are now an expert on missiles? And our cables are not safe?" He continues, "Mr. Volkov, your research is lacking some important and pertinent information. Do you know what a shielded cable is?" Lieutenant Volkov does not respond, and now Mr. Orlov is smiling. "It is when a special insulating factor is put in the cable so that it cannot be tapped, including the inductive mode. We have one here at our KGB headquarters, and it runs to the Kremlin. And I have been informed by Mr. Orlov that our cable in the Sea of Okhotsk is also shielded and cannot be tapped, again not even by this inductive mode." Mr. Orlov nods his head in agreement.

Lieutenant Volkov responds, "Mr. Sokolov, I am not sure what to say to this. But I can assure you, no one ever said anything to me about 'shielded' cables."

"I am sure of it. Like I said, you could have done more research. And this American submarine you wanted us to look into—I believe it is called a flat fish or something?"

"*Halibut* is its name," interjects Volkov.

"Well, you were partially right. It does have a large complement of divers who do this diving for extended periods of time. But not, as you fancifully imagined, for wiretaps. They were instead interested in our cruise missiles on the bottom of the sea. We have a splash zone in the Sea of Okhotsk where we test such missiles. And that is what the Americans have been interested in."

"But how do you know this?" asks Lieutenant Volkov.

"It is above your pay grade, Volkov."

"At any rate, even if the Americans could locate these cruise missiles, they will not find anything of value. When they crash into the sea, they break up into thousands of pieces. And about this Mr. Pelton—you had no reservations about him?" Lieutenant Volkov is now not certain how to respond. "It never occurred to you that he could be playing you?"

"Playing me?" Volkov utters in surprise.

"How much did you pay him for this information?" asks Mr. Sokolov.

"Just 35,000 American dollars. I can assure you this is a very modest sum for this sort of information."

"So we got a bargain?" says Mr. Sokolov sarcastically, while Mr. Orlov chuckles.

"Lieutenant Volkov, in all the interviews you and your subordinates did with this Mr. Pelton, did he ever present you with any documents? He gave you no documentation, *did he?!* All he told you of the NSA and everything else is what he wanted you to believe. It seems you were eating right out of his hand and paying him to do this."

Lieutenant Volkov responds, "Sir, I still believe my basic conclusions are right."

"Yes, you do, and that is why you will be reporting to Mr. Orlov from now on. He is involved in our security equipment. He is an expert on these sorts of things. He is also the one who brought your failures to my attention. You have a big imagination, Volkov, possibly useful. You were lucky about the destroyer, or it could have been worse for you. So I am willing to give you another chance after more maturing."

"Now all, I repeat, *all*, of your travels and phone calls will first be checked by Mr. Orlov. You will report to him and follow his advice. Follow it to the letter!"

"But you have the wrong impression …"

Mr. Sokolov again waves his hand to stop Lieutenant Volkov from talking. "That will be all, Lieutenant Volkov. Good day."

After Lieutenant Volkov leaves the office, Mr. Sokolov shakes his head in disgust and says to Mr. Orlov, "Keep me abreast of his progress."

Chapter XXVIII
Icing on the Cake!

The success of this mission brought a joy to many, and even little pieces of information were passed along to share in the success of it. There was also an excitement about letting those in the States know that it was a success, as they were waiting in anticipation of our mission's results. After leaving the Sea of Okhotsk, *Halibut* was a full ten days out in the Pacific before a radio message was sent with a simple, "USS *Halibut*, all is success!"

It was a bright sunny day when our sub and crew safely returned to San Francisco Bay. As the *Halibut* approaches the Golden Gate Bridge, a huge sign made by the wives of the submariners could be seen hanging from it: "Welcome Home USS *Halibut!*"

Right under the Golden Gate, while still in route to Mare Island, the *Halibut* was met by a naval vessel that came alongside to receive our recordings. The recordings had been placed in plastic bags in case they fell overboard.

Those from the naval vessel who took the recordings were armed and had on bulletproof vests. These guards were scurrying around the deck of the *Halibut* with their eyes wide open, as if to make sure they had everything. Quite a contrast from us as we were tired from our long deployment and had climbed up out of the inside of the *Halibut*. To these guards we must have looked like albino rats coming out of a cave.

We sat on the deck looking at San Francisco and enjoying the sun. Before the guards shoved off, they unloaded several boxes of fresh fruit that was passed around to all the crew.

Captain Larson and the project officer were on the deck of the *Halibut*, and were watching the navy's guards unload the recordings.

The project officer said, "Good to breathe fresh air again after 96 days."

"They don't even want to wait until we make port to get our recordings," said the captain.

Project Officer responded, "The CIA and NSA are ecstatic. They know we recorded two-way communications.

"Captain, I have to remain with the recordings. I will be flying out from Alameda Naval Air Station. Before the sun goes down today, I and the recordings will both be in Washington, D.C.

"That hard, white plastic core that was found during the dives was from the inside of the Russian cable. I even found a picture of it in the Soviet's own reference books of their cables. I know what its capabilities are, and in all probability, we now know more about this cable than the ones who are using it in Siberia.

"I have to shove off now."

The captain and the project officer saluted each other and parted.

Exceeding Expectations

This operation turned out to be the Mount Everest of spy missions. And to my knowledge has never been equaled. We were spies with front-row seats in the Soviet headquarters, listening to all their uncensored calls to Moscow. And this went on for a decade! In short, we learned how they thought, and this is still valuable today. Captain Larson told us divers that at the debriefing he gave of our mission, two admirals told him it was the best operation they had ever heard of.

Some of the recordings were only a sailor calling his sweetheart or a general talking to his mistress, but much of it was important military secrets.

CIA Release

The CIA released that our nuclear submarines were able to tap Soviet underwater cables "submarines … were able to intercept high-level military messages." (Declassified in Part—Sanitized Copy Approved for Release

2012/05/08:   CIA-RDP90-
00965R000605140016-2)

CIA Release

"Ivy Bells, allowed the United States to intercept messages that Soviet submarines sent to military command posts ashore when they returned to their harbors after sea cruises. Among other things, the messages included information about where the Soviets subs had been and what they had done." (Declassified in Part—Sanitized Copy Approved for Release 2012/02/24:   CIA-RDP90-00965R000403270006-3)

The intelligence gleaned from Operation Ivy Bells aided our arms negotiators and led directly to the SALT II talks in 1979. Many believe it helped bring about the end of the Cold War. It can be debated how much help this operation was in ending the Cold War, but it did have a part. It must have been very frustrating for the Soviets when they found out that we knew every secret they sent through these cables. All their plans were being read by the CIA, and we would have countered their weapons and countermeasures. And at that time they were going broke trying to keep pace with America. Giving up on the Cold War probably seemed like a good idea, and then the Soviet Union collapsed.

One of the things that was said to have come from these cable taps was that we learned the Soviets were more afraid of us than we were of them. They feared a nuclear first strike by the USA, and thereafter we postured ourselves to ease the tensions between us.

Author receiving plaque from Captain Charles R. Larson. Commanding Officer of the USS Halibut 587. Captain Larson later became a four-star admiral and was given command of

the entire Pacific. Born November 20, 1936—
Died July 26, 2014.

Legion of Merit

I was awarded the Legion of Merit for
this dive, along with all the divers who entered
the water.

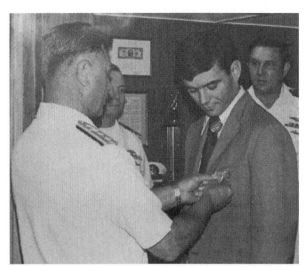

About eight months after I was out of the navy a congressional committee approved my Legion of Merit. I returned to Point Loma for a brief ceremony and a two star admiral pinned the medal on.

The commendation I received reads: "SW2 [DV] Garry M. Matheny, USN. Deployed for a second and even more arduous deployment. During this 96-day deployment he participated in a submarine operation of great importance to the government of the United States. Although description of this operation is precluded by security constraints, the ratee performed in a hostile environment under great operational stress requiring exceptional courage, constant vigilance and keen professional competence. His performance in that environment was superb and was a key factor in the ship's success in that operation." It was signed by C. R. Larson, Capt. USN Commanding Officer.

Thank You, Lord!

After my last water entry in Siberia, things changed for me. I was glad I had helped my country, but I had also accomplished my personal goal of making this dive, and everything else seemed small in comparison. Other things that were important seemed secondary.

I had done what others had wanted to do, though I can't say I deserved it more than they did. God had allowed me to do what I dreamed of. The cards were not stacked against me, and I would not have to always "sit on the bench" and think life was passing me by. I had a smile in my heart. The only catch was, we could not tell anyone about it, because we had all signed nondisclosure acts. Still, even that did not seem to matter. I'd been able to do my heart's desire.

In truth, these dives should not have been so important to me, but they were. They were more important than all the other times I have been passed over or blocked from doing what I had wanted. And yes, I had a big head about it. But something had changed. I no longer felt the need to prove myself, but instead I saw the need to please the Lord. And for the first time, I thanked the Lord that He did not let me die in that car wreck.

I am thankful to all those who were watching out for our country and had a part in making it possible: NSA, CIA, and the US Navy. But God allowed it, and He can allow your dreams also. Of course, God may say no, many times I have not received what I asked for. Still He wants us to look to Him in prayer for our dreams. There are things God will not give us simply because we will not ask Him! The Bible says, "Ye have not, because ye ask not" (James 4:2). For some it's pride that keeps them from asking God. "I don't need any help" is their attitude. There are some things you could have had already in your life, but you have not asked Him. So, "Ye have not, because ye ask not." Why haven't you asked God? You don't want to get your heart right with Him? You forgot? Lack of faith? When I get to heaven, the last thing I would want to hear is, "See all these things I wanted to give you while you were on Earth, *but you forgot to ask!*" And if God gives us something, He expects us to use it for Him.

A month after returning to the States, I completed my time in the navy, was honorably discharged, and from there I went straight to Bible college.

"Why go to Bible college? Is not God big enough to bless your ministry without that?"

Question: How do you become a navy diver? Answer: You start by joining the navy! I would not call boot camp fun, but I would never have become a navy diver without it. There is a logical progression of the training you need to reach the goals you want. If you are not willing to learn from others or if you have too much pride to place yourself under other people's authority, then you will end up with unfulfilled dreams. One may have zeal, but without proper training, he is no better than an unguided missile. There are prices we pay for the dreams we want.

I also, with the Lord's help, at least up to now, have been keeping my decision to serve the Lord, which I made while I was in Siberia. After graduation from Bible college, I served as associate pastor and then pastor in the state of Washington for a total of 12 years. Since 1991, my wife and I have been missionaries in the country of Romania.

Bittersweet

Even before *Halibut*'s last deployment, all on board knew that it was her last run—because she had come to the end of her nuclear fuel.

Captain Larson presided at her decommissioning with about 500 people present. Many people I have never met worked behind the scene to develop the innovative technology of the USS *Halibut*, and they also share in her remarkable success. *Halibut*'s awards from this and her other missions, which were also great, were acknowledged at this ceremony. I was in summer school at Bible college when she was decommissioned, but my heart was there. Those I talked to who were there said it was emotional and several had teary eyes.

Presidential Unit Citations

While the USS *Halibut* was still in service, she had the distinction of being the most highly decorated submarine of the post-WWII era. In 1968 the USS *Halibut* received the first of her Presidential Unit Citations. Many people are aware of the mission to recover the sunken Soviet submarine K-129, known as Project Azorian (the press called it "Jennifer"). In 1974 the *Hughes Glomar Explorer* recovered at least part of this Soviet submarine. However, this Soviet sub was not found by the *Hughes Glomar Explorer* but by the USS *Halibut*.

The *Halibut* had found K-129 using her Fish. The Russians had searched for their lost sub for several months but were unsuccessful; however, the *Halibut* found K-129 in only three weeks, and that at a depth of over three miles, a feat nothing less than spectacular.

President Nixon personally presented this award to the crew of the USS *Halibut*. This ceremony was conducted in secret so the news media would not ask questions as to why he was there.

In 1972 the USS *Halibut* received yet another Presidential Unit Citations for Operation Ivy Bells. After this it was deemed too risky to continue to award her these citations. *Halibut* was, after all, a spy sub, and the attention these Presidential Unit Citations were drawing to the *Halibut* was not welcome. Both Presidential Unit Citations, the one for Project Azorian, and the one for Operation Ivy Bells, are found in the epilogue.

Farewell to Our Sub, the USS *Halibut*!

Most of the submariners and saturation divers on the *Halibut* knew they would never again be involved in such a special operation. Some on the *Halibut* were "lifers" (20 or more years on active duty), but most of us were only in the navy for four to six years. We came from many different states and backgrounds, and the navy trained and formed us into an effective force. Then we were discharged to return to our own hometowns, never to see each other again.

We have all seen those who wear ball caps with the name of their duty station or their ship's name written on it. Sometimes it will say "WWII Veteran" or "Pearl Harbor Survivor." They are rightly proud of their service and we salute them! And those of us involved with Operation Ivy Bells also had a mission, a purpose, and a goal, which we accomplished and had exceeded expectations. It was a true adventure, and we were having the time of our life. But then it was stamped "TOP SECRET" and remained under this seal for the next four decades. One diver jokingly said, "Hey, guys, I am a national hero, but I can't tell anybody about it!"

There were times when we were back in

the States, in a store or walking down a street, when a diver would say with glee, "They don't know. None of these people know what we have done." Please forgive our bragging, but we had no one else we could talk to about it. Even today almost no one has heard of saturation diving, and most still have no idea what the US Navy pulled off.

Near to where the *Halibut* docked from her last patrol, her sister ship was tied up. This was the sub that would take *Halibut*'s place, she was better equipped and had a few modifications helpful for the divers. The crew of this sister ship were getting ready for their patrol, and they walked about with a determination to get the job done, as did the sub that would follow them. But at that time the *Halibut* was waiting to become scrap metal.

She was mothballed in Washington State, her reactor was removed, and she was struck from the Naval Vessel Register. Later she was disposed of and cut up for her HY-80 steel. Today there is no USS *Halibut*; she exists only in pictures and the memories of sailors. She was decommissioned at Mare Island, California. After 1,232 dives, *Halibut*'s colors were lowered for the last time on June 30, 1976.

Other submarines would later continue what the *Halibut* had started, and we can be proud of their accomplishments, which were no less important and needed. But it was the USS *Halibut* that led the way. *Farewell to a great submarine!*

My Gift to Dad

My wife, Nancy and I both want to shine for Jesus Christ and are thankful that He has allowed us to be missionaries among the gracious Romanian people. But my greatest mission challenge has been my dad.

Once, when I was witnessing to some old friends, one said, "You like to bug your dad about this salvation thing, don't you?"

I responded, "Yes, I don't want my dad to die and go to hell and burn."

There is no other man on this planet that I loved more than my dad and I had decided that if my dad did not go to heaven, it would not be because I was too afraid to witness to him. My mom did not get saved till she was 86 years old. I led her to the Lord over the phone from Romania. But my dad was not saved, and I had to try to reach him for Christ.

When my dad was 94 years old, while I was home on furlough from Romania, I went to visit him in a veteran's rest home in Minneapolis, Minnesota. On the third day of our visit, I rolled his wheelchair outside and shared with him something I had never told him before.

And of some have compassion, making a difference. (Jude 1:22)

Author witnessing to his dad.

"Dad, you remember me going into the Seabees for the navy, don't you?"

"Well, yes, and I was glad you went in the service, son. That was the best thing for you."

"Yes, it was. And you remember when I became a diver and then a saturation diver and I was on that submarine the USS *Halibut*?"

"Of course I do, Garry. I was very proud of you."

"I know, and I am glad. One more thing. Do you know why I did all that?"

He pulled his head back and shrugged his shoulders.

"Well, I did it for you. All that was for you Dad. Don't get me wrong; I really enjoyed it. And I am so thankful to God that he let me do all that. But my decision to go into the military in the first place was to please you."

I then told him how I had made that decision while in the hospital because of my car wreck, and I had seen how disappointed he was in me. And because of that I wanted to do something that would make him happy. When I was telling him this, I also shared how I had trusted Jesus Christ as my Savior while I was in the navy.

Then I asked him, "Dad, did you know that was my reason for going into the navy?"

"I knew you were in the navy on that submarine, but no, not that part you shared about why you did it."

"Well, that is how it happened. I did it all for you." I paused momentarily and then asked him one more time, "Dad, would you like Jesus Christ to be your Savior?"

He then simply said, "Yes."

I asked him if he would take his cap off, because we were going to talk to the One who made us. I asked him to repeat the following prayer after me but to say it back to God in heaven. The words in themselves have no magic in them, but if one prays them from his heart to God, He will hear and save that soul.

Could *you* pray from your heart the following prayer? God promises to save all who will do this. *"For whosoever shall call upon the name of the Lord shall be saved"* (Romans 10:13).

"<u>Dear God, I believe, that your Son, Jesus Christ, died on the cross and that on the third day his body arose from the grave. And now I ask Him to save me. Dear Jesus, thank you for taking my place on the cross and paying for my sins. Please come into my heart and save me, and when I die, take me to heaven. In Jesus's name.</u>"

I have led people to the Lord for over 40 years. But my dad did something when he was praying that I had never heard before. He called God "Sir." This won't mean much to others, but knowing my dad and how sparingly he used the word "sir," I knew it was his highest form of respect.

"Dad, you meant that, didn't you?"

"Well, of course I meant it!" he said. "A man would have to be a [blankety-blank] fool not to do something like that!" He didn't know not to use those "adjectives," but I was smiling anyway.

I'm Glad

The fifth commandment says, *"Honour thy father and thy mother."* And God is faithful to His promise that is attached to this commandment, *"that it may go well with thee"* (Deuteronomy 5:16). Just as setting out to please my dad had made me happy, so setting out to please God has made Nancy and me very happy!

I had almost completely block this mission out of my mind. I was not against it, but after all, I could not talk of it, so why think about it? Then I found out the CIA had dozens of these reports in their FOIA reading room. Going over them, and especially writing about this great adventure, brought back all sorts of memories and feelings I had as a young man.

I realize now I am to please the Lord not prove myself. Looking back at that time period I see a young man who needed more courage to live for God. And God brought Christians around to encourage me. Reminiscing about it moved my heart. God had blessed me, and I thanked Him for it.

I celebrated my 25th birthday in Siberia while on the sixth day of our saturation dive. I made over 300 dives in the navy. Now I am 69 and have made only six dives since I left the navy. It is a chapter in my life that closed a long time ago, but I enjoyed going over it very much. I am truly thankful for that great experience, but one can't live in the past. That mission was used by God to turn over to Him what I would do with my life. And I'm glad I gave that decision to Him, not wasting my life on myself but I gave it to Christ!

Epilogue

Why the Red Light?

As to why the Red Light came on in my helmet, this happened to another diver on one of the earlier training dives. And both situations were determined to be leaking fittings on the come-home bottle.

Why Was I Jerked Backward?

When I returned to the dive chamber, I should have gone on the outside of the first leg of the DSRV because when I had entered the water, that was the side I was on. But instead I went on the other side and, as a result, wrapped my umbilical cord around this metal leg. Because of this, every time the tenders pulled on my umbilical to bring me back into the dive chamber, it had the opposite effect and I was pulled backward away from where I needed to go. And when I pulled up my umbilical cable, it was pulled out of the hands of the tenders. In essence we were playing tug-of-war with my umbilical cable, though at the time neither the tenders or I knew it.

Relic of the Cold War

"The Beast"

CIA Release

"Pelton had compromised a costly, long-running and highly sophisticated electronic eavesdropping operation involving U. S. Submarines and a high technology device that officials now believe is in Soviet hands." (Declassified in Part—Sanitized Copy

The navy also developed a device, a Pod, or "Beast" as it was called, about three feet in diameter by 20 feet long. It could be left behind after a sub left the Sea of Okhotsk and continue to store recordings. It was able to store a year's worth of information and was kept running by a mini nuclear reactor (plutonium-238).

This Pod was found by the Russians and placed on public display in Russia's Great Patriotic War Museum in Moscow. Soviet Vice Admiral Alexander Zhardetsky, former head of Military Intelligence, said many transistors inside this device were stamped "Made in the USA." Once the Russians found out about Operation Ivy Bells, they would no longer transmit their intelligence in the same way.

This Pod worked well on the surface but kept malfunctioning at depth. Before I was attached to the *Halibut*, I had seen the device, and the barge I was then assigned to gave support to those who were trying to solve the problem. It is my understanding that the *Halibut* tried to use it before I was assigned to her, but it was not used when we dove in 1975. However, it was used in subsequent missions and apparently worked well until the operation was betrayed.

The Cable Taps Ended

The cable recordings continued after I left the navy in 1975 and remained safe until the 1980s, when it was compromised.

In 1980 when Pelton first informed the Russians, they did not immediately search for the device. Different theories exist as to why the Russians waited. Some believe that after Pelton informed the Russians, they may have fed us disinformation. If that were so, then why did the Russians recover the Pod and stop the taps? If they wanted to give us false information, it would have been to their advantage to keep it going.

It seems more likely that at the beginning, without another corroborating source, Pelton's story may not have received attention at a high level.

CIA Release

Deputy CIA Director Robert M. Gates, when talking about the Pelton case, said, "Whether you're a Soviet or an American intelligence officer, you often won't take at face value what you hear from a single source …" (Declassified and Approved for Release 2013/05/21: CIA-RDP99-01448R000301220033-5)

Also, for much of the year this sea cannot be navigated by surface vessels. According to *New World Encyclopedia,* "In winter, navigation on the Sea [of Okhotsk] is difficult, if not impossible, due to the formation of large ice floe. … Between October and April, temperatures are bitter, and the area is ice-covered. …" But in 1981 our satellites saw a Soviet salvage vessel at the site of the taps. The navy sent one of our project subs to the site to see if the taps were still working, but that was when we learned the Pod was missing, the Russians had it!

Cover Story

The cover story of recovering debris from the Soviet cruise missiles was actually carried out by the USS *Halibut*. This was done before I was assigned to the *Halibut* in 1974. A saturation diver told me that when *Halibut* returned to America, she was "parked" offshore near San Diego and close to the Point Loma sub base. At night divers from the *Halibut* detached an undercarriage that was attached to the bottom of our sub and moved it close to shore. There the contents (broken pieces of the supersonic Russian SS-N-12 Sandbox missile) were transferred to a waiting truck.

In order to keep from widening the circle of those who knew about the operation, the navy used saturation divers to drive the truck. The SAT diver who drove the truck told me he felt like James Bond when he took bags from divers coming out of the water and then hurriedly placed them in the back of a tarp-covered truck. These pieces were then transferred to a navy research laboratory to make a countermeasure against this missile. It was discovered that the Soviets were only using a radar guidance system, not an infrared system.

Presidential Unit Citation—1968

"For exceptional meritorious service on support of National Research and Development efforts while serving as a unit in the Submarine Force, U.S. Pacific Fleet. Conducting highly technical submarine operations, over an extended period of time, USS *HALIBUT* (SSN-587) successfully concluded several missions of significant scientific value to the Government of the United States. The professional, military, and technical competence, and inspiring devotion to duty of *HALIBUT's* officers and men, reflect great credit upon themselves and the United States Naval Service."

Presidential Unit Citation—1972

"For extraordinary heroism and outstanding performance of duty as a unit in the Submarine Force, United States Pacific Fleet during 1972, USS *HALIBUT* successfully accomplished two highly productive and complex submarine operations of immeasurable value to the Government of the United States.

The superb professional competence, extremely effective teamwork and exemplary devotion to duty displayed by the officers and men of USS *HALIBUT* reflect great credit upon themselves, the Submarine Force and the United States Naval Service."

History

The USS *Halibut* was commissioned on January 4, 1960, and was originally designated SSGN. (*SS* is *submarine*, *G* is *guided missile*, and *N* is *nuclear powered*.) She was designed to launch Regulas I and II cruise missiles. On March 25, 1960, she became the first nuclear-powered submarine to launch a guided missile. She continued in this role until replaced by the Polaris submarines.

In 1965 *Halibut* underwent a major overhaul for special operations and was designated attack submarine SSN-587. Submarines are normally classified into two categories: *boomers* and *fast attacks*. The boomer is a ballistic-missile submarine, and fast attacks either protect carrier groups or go on special missions.

In 1968 the *Halibut* was again given a major overhaul and equipped with side-look sonar, a mainframe computer, and seabed skids so she could sit on the ocean floor. She was also given a saturation-diving chamber, or habitat, for deep dives.

Looking for the Amplifier

There were two deployments of the *Halibut* in 1974. The second one, which I was on, made no saturation dives but only looked for the "amplifier" that was on the Russian cable. Up until this time we had only gotten one-way communications from the Soviets. When the divers placed the tapping devices on the cable, only the communication from one direction was strong enough to be picked up by our recordings. We needed to find this amplifier to get signals strong enough to record the conversations going in both directions.

The search for this amplifier was not simple, with our sub fighting currents and moving at a snail's pace in order for the Fish to follow the cable. Sand covered this cable in many places, and the cable itself was not always laid in a straight line. The Soviet ship that replaced this amplifier, after finishing the job, did not drop it directly on top of the cable that was below on the seafloor but laid it off to one side. That meant the full 400 feet of the cable, the distance from the seabed floor to the surface, was pulled to one side and dropped overboard. So every time our Fish passed over this section of cable, one leg did veer off, but the Fish picked up the other side only a few feet away as it was coming out of the sand. They naturally thought the cable was still running in basically a straight line, but it was not, and this was the section the amplifier was on. This section was eventually searched, and there they found the amplifier. Without the side thrusters, this would not have been possible.

To God be the glory!
If this book has been a blessing to you,
please encourage others to read it. And pray
that God will use it to reach others.

Sites by G. M. Matheny

True Christian Short Stories. Read for *FREE*, and besides short stories, this site has books and articles by this author.

http://www.truechristianshortstoriesfreebygmmatheny.com/

Besides English, this site is also in,

Spanish, Pequeñas Historias Cristianas - Home
http://www.pequeashistoriascristianasporgmmatheny.com/

Romanian, Scurte Povestiri Creştine de G. M. Matheny
http://www.scurte-povestiri.com/

French, Petites Histoires Chrétiennes Vraies - ACCUEIL
http://www.petites-histoires-chrtiennes-vraies-pargmmatheny.com/

Chinese (Mandarin),

真实的基督信仰小故事 http://www.gmmatheny.com/

The Layman's Biblical Handbook. For *FREE*, this site covers more than 200 biblical subjects.

http://www.thelaymansbiblicalhandbook.com/

Besides English it is also in,

Spanish http://www.manualbiblico.com/

Romanian

http://www.471633614246918175.com

Books by GM Matheny

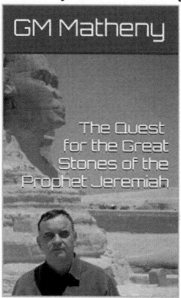

The Quest for the Great Stones of the Prophet Jeremiah. Read for *FREE*.
https://www.truechristianshortstoriesfreebygmmatheny.com/the-quest-for-the-great-stones-of-the-prophet-jeremiah.html

The first in our Quest Series.

Stories about mystery or adventure have planted the thought that you have to be single and chasing your girlfriend to have any fun, and at the end of the story the couple embrace, kiss, and then on the screen or the printed page, appears "The End." The unspoken thought is, when you settle down and get married, the fun is over.

My wife, Nancy, our son Caleb, and myself, with Jesus Christ as our leader, made our own "special ops team," gathered "intelligence," and set off on an adventure of discovery! This took place between February 2005 and October 2008 and shows how Christians armed with the Bible found what the scholars could not.

What others are saying. "Garry Matheny makes a terrific adventure story out of just two verses in the Old Testament book of Jeremiah. The amateur sleuth beats some of the world's top archaeologists at their own game, and you get to go along for the ride. You'll enjoy it!"
In both paperback and Kindle.
https://www.amazon.com/dp/1981082832

The Quest for the Red Sea Crossing
The second in our Quest Series and should be read before our book *The Quest for Mount Sinai.*
Read for *FREE*
https://www.truechristianshortstoriesfreebygm matheny.com/the-quest-for-the-red-sea-crossing.html

Did the ancient Egyptians leave an account of the Red Sea (Yam Suf) crossing? Most people who have studied this would respond, "But the ancient Egyptians never monumentalized their defeats." Yes, and today no one is expecting to find an ancient Egyptian inscription that says, "The God of the Hebrew slaves beat us up." However, there is an Egyptian legend (not the el-Arish Shrine) that does more than just lend itself to the sea crossing by Israel. It is about a battle between two Egyptian "gods," and in this battle, the "good god," who represents Egypt, loses (something very rare), and the "bad god," who represents the foreigners, wins, and it takes place at the bottom of the sea! And what is of more interest is that this takes place right in front of the four place names of the Red Sea/Yam Suf crossing, as given in Exodus 14:2! (Pi-hahiroth, Migdol, Baal-zephon, and "the sea.") But because this Egyptian legend was said to have happened in an unexpected location, it has been passed over.

Both paperback and Kindle.

https://www.amazon.com/dp/1982966114

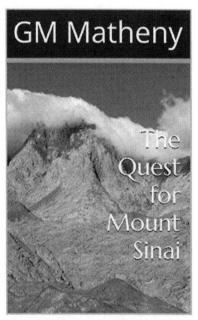

The Quest for Mount Sinai
The third in our Quest Series.
A pharaoh of Egypt went to Mount Sinai
and engraved his named there!

In December 2013, two years after our book was first published, an inscription made by a pharaoh of Egypt was found at the mountain that I have proposed as Mount Sinai. And more than a hundred years ago, a hieroglyphic inscription was found in the East Nile Delta, also made by a king of Egypt, describing an expedition to a location the scholars have hotly debated. But the location is now confirmed, for the same king made both inscriptions, and he found something there that Israel left at Mount Sinai.

This one is presently on sell for .99 cents!

Both paperback and Kindle.

https://www.amazon.com/dp/1983006815

https://www.amazon.com/dp/B07DBF8TYV

71325817R00165

Made in the USA
Columbia, SC
25 August 2019